COLLECTED POEMS

Rowan Williams was born in 1950. He was the 104th Archbishop of Canterbury (2002–2012). He spent much of his earlier career as an academic at the Universities of Cambridge and Oxford successively. Williams stood down as Archbishop of Canterbury on 31 December 2012 and became Master of Magdalene College at Cambridge University in January 2013 retiring in 2020. Carcanet reissued *The Poems of Rowan Williams* in April 2014.

Collected Poems

ROWAN WILLIAMS

CARCANET POETRY

First published in Great Britain in 2021 by
Carcanet
Alliance House, 30 Cross Street
Manchester, M2 7AQ
www.carcanet.co.uk

A CIP catalogue record for this book is
available from the British Library.

ISBN 978 1 80017 109 1

Book design by Andrew Latimer
Printed in Great Britain by SRP Ltd, Exeter, Devon

The publisher acknowledges financial
assistance from Arts Council England.

CONTENTS

The Poems of Rowan Williams (2014)

Headwaters (2008)

The Other Mountain (2014)

New Poems

GWEN JOHN IN PARIS[1]
for Celia

I

I am Mrs Noah: my clothes-peg head
pins sheets out between showers;
in my clean cabin, my neat bed,
the bearded Augusti lumber in and out.

I am Mrs Noah: I call the beasts home
together, the cat to lie down with the slug,
the nun with the flapper. I comb
the hair of ferns to dry on deck.

I am Mrs Noah: arranging the flowers
in bright dust round my garden shed,
I watch the silent sky without doubt,
in the soaked moonlit grass sleep without dread.

I am Mrs Noah: the blossoms in the jug
throw their dense pollen round the stormy room like foam;
my hands hold beasts and friends and light in check,
shaping their own thick gauzy rainbow dome.

II

Rodin's fingers: probe, pinch, ease open,
polish, calm. Keep still, he says,
recueille-toi: sit on the rock,
gaze out to sea, and I shall make you
patience on a monument. Keep still.
I kept still; he looked away.
On the stairs. In the yard. I stood,
not noticed, in the middle of half-broken stone,
aborted figures. I was a failed work,
keeping still among the darting birds.
His hand refused to close, my lips
stayed open all hours. He might drop in.

Brushing against Rilke in the corridor:
he smiles with fear or pity. Angels,
polished and black, bump into us
at strange angles. Afternoon light
swells like a thundercloud in the attic, busy
around an empty chair, draped like the dead king's throne.

III

Thérèse dreamed that her father
stood with his head wrapped
in black, lost.

Thérèse looks at the photographer
under his cloth and sees
Papa not seeing her.

I watch Thérèse watching
Papa and wondering
whenthe cloth comes off.

I watch her thinking
you can spend a short life
not being seen.

Thérèse looks at me and says,
Only when you can't see him do you
know you're there.

She says, Can you see me
not seeing you? That's when
you see me.

---

1 Gwen John made numerous sketches from photographs of St Thérèse of
Lisieux as a child.

IV

I sent the boys off with their father.
I shall wait on the drenched hill.
Meudon, my Ararat, where the colours pour
into the lines of a leaf's twist.
And the backs of the chairs and schoolgirls' plaits at Mass
are the drawn discord, expecting
the absolution of light in the last bar.

DRYSTONE

In sooty streams across the hill, rough, bumpy,
contoured in jagging falls and twists, they walk
beyond the crest, beyond the muddy clough,
children's coarse pencil sentences, deep-scored,
staggering across a thick absorbing sheet, dry frontiers
on a wet land, dry streams across wet earth,
coal-dry, soot-dry, carrying the wind's black leavings
from the mill valley, but against the gales
low, subtle, huddling: needs more than wind to scatter them.

There is no glue, there is no mortar, subtle,
solid enough for here: only the stained air blowing
up from the brewery through the lean dry gaps;
hard to know how an eye once saw the consonance,
the fit of these unsocial shapes, once saw
each one pressed to the other's frontier, every one
inside the other's edge, and conjured the dry aliens
to run, one sentence scrawled across the sheet,
 subtle against the wind, a silent spell, a plot.

SIX O'CLOCK

As the bird
rides up the sky, the last sun
looking up gilds in the hollows
of the wings, an afterthought of gift
 to guests ignored and hurt, but no,
the bird rides up the sky, eyes on the night.

When the sun
levels its sights across the grass,
it packs the blades and little animals
so tight, so heavy that you wonder
why they don't tumble over
into their new, uncompromising shadow,
into their inner dark.

OUR LADY OF VLADIMIR [1]

Climbs the child, confident,
up over breast, arm, shoulder;
while she, alarmed by his bold thrust
into her face, and the encircling hand,
looks out imploring fearfully
and, O, she cries, from her immeasurable eyes,
O how he clings, see how
he smothers every pore, like the soft
shining mistletoe to my black bark,
she says, I cannot breathe, my eyes
are aching so.

The child has overlaid us in our beds,
we cannot close our eyes,
his weight sits firmly,
fits over heart and lungs,
and choked we turn away
into the window of immeasurable dark
to shake off the insistent pushing warmth;
0 how he cleaves, no peace
tonight my lady in your bower,
you, like us, restless with bruised eyes
and waking to

a shining cry on the black bark of sleep.

---

[1] The icon of Our Lady probably dates from the twelfth century, and is preserved
in Moscow.

ADVENT CALENDAR

He will come like last leaf's fall.
One night when the November wind
has flayed the trees to bone, and earth
wakes choking on the mould,
the soft shroud's folding.

He will come like frost.
One morning when the shrinking earth
opens on mist, to find itself
arrested in the net
of alien, sword-set beauty.

He will come like dark.
One evening when the bursting red
December sun draws up the sheet
and penny-masks its eye to yield
the star-snowed fields of sky.

He will come, will come,
will come like crying in the night,
like blood, like breaking,
as the earth writhes to toss him free.
He will come like child.

RETURN JOURNEY

Why are places not neutral?
on the smoky screen of walls,
shop windows, sky and pavement spin
the flickering reels of evidence, dust crawling up
the frames, the privately detected chronicle
of clumsily arranged affairs with time and place.

Grace, yes, but damnation too dissolves
in place, so it is not the future
but the past we know to be incredible,
eluding the imagination: unmoved mover
of uncomprehending souls, shaping the mind
glued to the dusty and unwelcome screen.

Push up the blinds and in the room
nothing has gone, there in the dark
we sit unmovable, the wounds as fresh
as ever, all that was ever done
frozen against the walls in a bright moment,
iron and bitter, bright like life.

Fresh from the freezer, all the smooth pain that settled,
stayed when we went on, sat and nestled,
patiently in the corner, waiting to be collected
when we happen back, it stares in silence
at these new, would-be alien selves,
a still, unsmiling, lifelike face.

While I sit mute, suspicious of my choice
(Reserve or fluency), how do I reach
You, then, across the acres of the room?
Yes, all the platitudes are clear enough:
Muteness is eloquence, silence is the stuff
Of sharing, while hands work a busy loom;
But on your flesh my hands will still be blind.
Your face is shut. Your body gives no voice,
But charts a distance. How do we avoid
A treaty with the compromising word?
Knowing that after, when we have destroyed
The ambiguity, the precious surd
Of uncommitted quiet, we shall find
Our honesty still waits to be aligned?

You smiled, apologising for the sound –
The hollow distant penetrating hum
Of a dim underground, fathoms down from us.
In those hard channels silence yields, not here;
Under the crust, a journey's length is clear.
The traveller there has mapped his terminus,
Watches for a predicted stop to come,
Steps in the floodstream, confidently bound
A foreknown distance. I cannot select
Periods so easy from the trodden edge
Of words in flux. Prospects of an unchecked,
Unending bursting into haemorrhage
Cut me a channel where we both, pulled down
Under the hollow humming wheels, shall drown.

Tell me what I am asking, then, what plea
You hear without pronouncing. It is you
Who hold the mirror and who know the name
And will not say it; while the desperate cold
Unchristened infant, years or seconds old,
Tries its new lungs with incoherent blame,
Clench-fisted, begs the necessary clue
That holds the hand of an identity
Its lifelong distance. Absolution's cheap
This way, as I laboriously forget
The guilt of joint conspirators, asleep
Against complaining noises, bodies set
Waiting for one to learn or one to teach:
Casual midwives for miscarrying speech.

Cracks open in the floor across the years.
The rumpled bed of stone shrugs off the heat
Of wooden coverlets, impatient with the dark,
And dust no longer binds the drifting blocks.
How long before the stone has forced the locks?
How long before the flesh has split the bark?
And the foundations, naked to our feet
Carry us stumbling on a bridge that clears
The dust-choked distance? While we wait to see
A waking earth that stirs into the sun,
Our covers still are drawn, the night walks free
Between our frontiers, where no path will run.
Under the wooden shroud, under the stone,
Under the dust, the fields are locked unsown.

The shifting floor, the smeared steps inlaid,
Loosened and footprinted with journey's scars,
Is this a field for growing, this a rock
For building? no: the sedges of a marsh
Where white horizons ring the eyes, and harsh
Bird cry scratches the standing pools, to shock
The marble dark in small and passing stars;
The flats of boring exigence displayed,
Unreckoned distance. This is all I make,
A roofless acting space, a voice exposed
To drop its crying in a careless lake
Of ragged eyes, of watchers undisposed
To see or pity stale romantic scenes
Decent embarrassment clothes with safety screens.

And if I told you, should I be surprised
If you, turning your head, asked me, And why?
The choice is mine, the landscape my design,
The black my painting, and the ice my chill;
Looked bitterly at the evasive skill
That locks me up inside this private sign,
Turning a greedy fascinated eye
On an emotion still uncompromised
At its still distance. If I do not tell,
And play under the bedclothes with conceits,
What prudence keeps me in this glassy cell,
The polished atoms of half-willed defeats?
Well, atoms split, my love, are lovers' death,
Out in the cold, no wind will lend us breath.

To break a lock by giving open tongue,
Stand up, come in and sing us out of doors,
I know stirs recollections in the flesh,
And blows the dust from pictures pushed away.
Collected shadows from another day –
Collected words, packed stinking, tight, unfresh,
Ready to send the shiver down old sores,
Echoes of other bodies, roundly flung
A few year's distance. And the hoarded tears,
Unheard reproaches, wait to be unlocked.
Meanwhile I thoughtfully deploy my fears,
Afraid to find my facile pities mocked,
Afraid my probing taps the blood again,
That my flesh too clouds over with the stain.

So did we ever have an assignation
Under the station clock? an intersection
Of complicated routes ? Was there a break
Between connections when we might have snatched a word,
Unusual and hard and timely, stirred
By urgencies too close for us to make
Excuses, plead appointments for protection,
Slew our eyes round, sketch a retreat formation
Into the distance promised by the hiss
And echo of things setting to depart
All round? Eyes scattering far and anxious not to miss
Something or anything; travelling apart.
You never came, we both of us could say,
Angry, relieved, rejected, gone away.

DEJEUNER SUR L'HERBE

Watching your hands
turn slenderly the glass
I wait for rim to snap
or bowl to spill;

but when it shall,
shall there be wine to drop
on the drab summer grass
or only hours' worth of spent sands?

TWELFTH NIGHT

In the clean winter pastures of the stars
is innocence, a soft and stinging dark
bathing the cataracted eyes
of age remembering.

In the dry winter chambers of the stars
is infancy, a soul unhistoried,
breathing new air, inheriting
no dead men's speech.

Old men live long between the stars:
where else is virgin earth for minds,
for memories bursting brown skins
and spilling seed?

Old men seek sleep between the stars,
cradles between the thin white fires
to rock away the scars of choice
to a bad dream.

O if we did not know,
then we should see the clean stars plain,
through the cool night, forgetting,
should come home.

O if we did not see,
then we should know the empty air,
the fields of sheep the fresh and unimagined
scents of spilled grass or leaf.

Now when the stars have called to welcome us,
how shall we not run home?
the far side of the desert promises
tearless childhood,

Now that the stars speak clear to us
the language of our marketplace, and cry
come buy, you poor, for innocence
is cheap tonight.

Journeys for old men are not kind
when comfort's sold to buy the single pearl;
yet the child's eye is lifetime's worth of gold,
world's worth of pilgrimage.

Journeys for old men are not mapped,
but for the backward lodestone of desire
for that oasis where the mind is quenched
under still leaves.

Once in the house we saw the trap:
their eyes told all, the childish mother
nursing the knowing mortal child,
a mocking boy.

Once in the house, the stars smiled back
pleased and sardonic at their wit;
sweet-baited lines that catch unpityingly
in the soft places.

Behind the stars no holiday,
no taking out of recollection, but
a cup pressed full of pasts
incalculable.

Behind the stars no happy end,
no dissolution of our scars,
no garden plot, no spilling grass:
the cot is empty.

Where has the child gone, to what fire,
what rubbish bin, what coins were laid
to close his eyes? give us at least
the choice of sending flowers.

Where has the child gone? is the watched sky
a single cenotaph for dead simplicity,
the stars a moss-grown requiescat
in half-remembered alphabets?

And we, conscripted mourners for the funeral,
hands full of soil, left sleepless
with the small corpse, until grey dawn
summons us out?

And we, the prisoners of a narrative
of deaths and soiling, heavy as the world,
of stale and endless air, of age,
scents of senility?

The child says, True, this market does not sell
forgetfulness. In a still pool
I hold a glass to all your storms,
to all your eyes.

The child says, True, for nothing is undone
beyond the stars, the tree that grows tonight
is hung with all the lives of men and women,
all your deaths.

You still are children, innocence not gone,
what memories of yours are worth the name?
where were you when the world's foundations
set in children's blood?

You still are children; all that you have known
is fear, not guilt, have felt the blade,
but not the handle of the moulder's knife
carving a mind.

Your histories belong to me; here is
not innocence but absolution, for
your scars are true, but I (always)
will bleed in them.

Your memories belong to me; I lie
awake at night and see for ever, while
the stars shall fall like leaves
to cover you.

GREAT SABBATH

Unwatched, the seventh dawn spreads,
Light smoothing out the sky, firm hands
Smearing a damp clay horizon-wide.
They wake, then lie unsurely side by side,
Knowing the ache and pull of novel bands,
The night's new memories grinding in their heads,

Not understood, their bodies newly strange.
Outside, the new light soaks the ground;
They chill, turn in towards each other's heat,
Then roll apart to test uncertain feet
On unknown earth. The dripping dawn around
Confirms the unformed fear. The world can change.

Outside, an absence. While they learned and slept,
It had drawn off behind the sky's stone face.
The world between their bodies and their palms
Is left to turn. The silence calms.
The morning's news is plain; the centre space
Is empty. Under the trees where he once stepped

It is for you to go. Under the gaping sky
You wake, he sleeps, you make, he lies at rest.
He will not come again; last night you made
A future he will not invade.
Today the sun is buried, unexpressed;
You shall shape how to live and how to die.

You shall make change. He leaves no room
For his own hand; you shall be history,
You shall build heaven, you shall quarry hell.
No one shall say you have (or not) made well.
And, bored and pious, talk of mystery,
When weeds are choking up his tomb.

We make, he sleeps. Only his bloody dreams
Tell him the works of freedom on the earth.
Your liberty his flight, your future and his death.
He dreams your hell for you to draw your breath,
Out of his emptiness he lets your birth,
It is his silence echoes back the screams.

For they have not forgotten everything;
They wake and lie unsurely side by side
And listen to a laboured, steady breath,
Insistent, unconsoled, remembered death.
A small-hours passing on the turning tide,
Alone and never taught what key to sing.

He will not come again, not in the form
He walked on your first earth. But will you know
Him when he slips, a dosser, through the door?
Oh yes. Who else will touch the raw
Salt, unhealed memory of worlds ago,
Whispering, once you knew, once you were warm.

Listen for promises, fantasize for care,
And you will fill the neutral sky with lead,
Make chains to stop the quiet flow of chance,
Sell all your working for a stripper's dance.
He chose his death; why can he not be dead,
And leave the bloody dreams at home elsewhere?

Drink up your tears; you can no longer need
The luxury of an old, cheap compassion.
To bury him may be a heavy cost,
But buys our future when today is lost,
Buys the clean stone from which we can refashion
Our image soiled by his remembered greed.

He asks his present back; the clay-daubed hands
Are picking at the dyke. Weep and you will unmix
The mortar, and the salt black sea will run
And catch and trip and drown us, one by one.
For walls are weaker than their strongest bricks.
Behind our stone, the moon-fed tide expands

To flood our fens. We walk with desperate care,
The locks are fragile and the wind is swelling,
Windows will rattle us awake, eyes wide,
To stare, lying unsurely side by side,
Quiet and fearful; there is no telling
What dreams will flesh out of the noisy air.

The stones had fallen down. We woke too late.
He has unlatched the house, smashed through the pains,
While we slept out our sixth and darkest night,
And taken back his gross seigneurial right.
Today he swills the cultivated plains,
Salting our clay; reclaiming our estate.

OYSTERMOUTH CEMETERY

Grass laps; the stone keels jar,
scratch quietly in the rippling soil.
The little lettered masts dip slowly
in a little breeze, the anchors here
are very deep among the shells.

Not till the gusty day
when a last angel tramples down
into the mud his dry foot hissing,
down to the clogged forgotten shingle,
till the bay boils and shakes,

Not till that day shall the cords snap
and all the little craft float stray
on unfamiliar tides, to lay their freight
on new warm shores, on those strange islands
where their tropic Easter landfall is.

THIRD STATION

Fall. And between the grey air
and your stone back will run the stream,
quick, cold, of weeping breath,
the mind's sour spit of overnight,
coating the broken skin against its load.

Lift. And between the stone spine
and the sun's weight are caught
the leavings of the mind, the grounds
that cloud the bottom of the heart and, shaken,
bitter it. Press to the sun your skin.

Turn. And between the weights of heaven and self
rub small the crying grain and burst
the puckered gelid streams. Wind tight the press
and mill our parching salt, our black and needful flour.
Bread. Tears.

Pillars of dusty air beneath the dome
of golden leaden sky strain to bear up
his sweaty heaviness, his bulging eyes
drawn inwards to their private pain,
his hands arthritic with those inner knots,
his blessings set aside.
He has forgotten us, this one,
and sees a black unvisitable place
where from all ages to all ages he will die
and cry, creating in his blood
congealing galaxies of heat and weight.
Why should he bless or need an open book?
we know the words as well as he,
the names, Alpha, Omega,
fire from fire, we know your cry
out of the dusty golden whirlwind, how you forget
us so that we can be.

---

[1] The mosaic of Christ the ruler of all in the monastery of Daphni, Greece.

AUGUSTINE

Take off your shoes,
paddle again in the hot dust.
My mother baked me on theses hot stones,
a foreign father handled, pressed
and broke and packed me back
to feed his furnaces
here on the baking dust.

Take down the curtains
round your hot bed.
The long moon shines away
back through the talking hours
of young men's faces damp with eloquence.
the midnight dust under the window
paints me my shadow, light and cold.

Take it and read.
Not now the child's lost voice
climbing the garden wall
in that exact and northern afternoon
to coax me into play. Take up
your shadow, read me
from the bakestone squares.

Take up the stones
and find the choked foundations.
My fingers push the dust away
from broken, staring faces,
half my heart. The world's mosaic
shattered for centuries in the sand
before my memory.

Take up your voice
and tell your shadow's story. If
I weave this web out of my belly,
spread it between the broken ribs
of the hot square, then shall I catch
the winged and stinging visitor,
breaker of each night's sleep?

Take off your shoes.
This dust is mine, this knotted web
is mine, this shadow
is my shape for you, and when
the hot dust scalds your eyes to tears,
who is it weeps with you to soak
your dust to speaking clay?

INDOORS

Beaten and close the earth in here,
small blunt old fingers day to day
packing the corners, moulding down serrated tops
along the walls; then pull and plait the springing brambles
into screens and springing grills, a scrollworked coverlet,
Sometimes the spines will catch, lift up a flake of settled skin,
sometimes a drop swells of small thin old blood. Or earth
runs in the cleft of a white hard old scar, mind wanders to
the recollected blow and bleeding, for an hour or two, from day to day,
whispering, familiar.

This is the house that years built, dropping soil
from the loose screes. Straddling the hill, the cottage sheds its tiles,
the books begin to corrugate with damp. Home
is the cleft where earth runs, and a little old thin blood,
home's where the hurt is, white and familiar as a bone.

RUBLEV[1]

One day, God walked in, pale from the grey steppe,
slit-eyed against the wind, and stopped,
said, Colour me, breathe your blood into my mouth.

I said, Here is the blood of all our people,
these are their bruises, blue and purple,
gold, brown, and pale green wash of death.

These (god) are the chromatic pains of flesh,
I said, I trust I make you blush,
0 I shall stain you with the scars of birth

For ever. I shall root you in the wood,
under the sun shall bake you bread
of beechmast, never let you forth

to the white desert, to the starving sand.
But we shall sit and speak around
one table, share one food, one earth.

---

[1] Andrei Rublev's icon showing the persons of the Trinity as angels
seated at a table dates from the fourteenth century and is in the
Tretyakov Gallery, Moscow.

SNOW FEN

On these drum-tight pegged flats, it does not fall
in blankets rucked around the soil,
soft fleece around the raw veins, no,
but drains away the colourblocks
leaving the pool of hollow bone.
It has called back the bleach, the chalk,
the pulse along a whistling buried wire
below the marsh, the monody,
bat-pitched, of the electric stars.

Sketches of street and hedge
and scribbled farms, the pencilled query notes
against the ledger, smear down steadily
to a grey page, rinsed at last
to its sharp grain again;
an unsuccessful cold and clichéd snap
soaks out, the canvas is tacked down
drum-tight and thirsty for the brush
of some less academic sky.

KETTLE'S YARD[1]
  4 March 1984

Pebbles and sea-light,
drift of grain across an ebbing floor,
land's end. The wind is sharp as gulls
past David's Pembroke window,
lettering the stars across
a winter wall.

The gods are grey
and concave, finger-printed into hollow eyes,
their stones warm ash. Fires on the shore
fold when the night drops and we build
the ferns to pack us warm
in crackling beds.

A bell for morning.
Pebbles at dawn push damp and black,
teasing awake. The wind is sharp as gulls,
so up the stairs: the sand swells round
a blunted skull. I wash
my face in stone.

---

[1] The unique 'domestic' Cambridge gallery established by David Jones's
friend Jim Ede.

Down in the small hollow where the currents shift
slowly, and drop with the thinning sun, the crows
float, crowding the shallow slopes of air,
and vague as specks of stubble fire: the sun
has scattered them from thinning flames, has clapped
a hollow hand, once, twice, a glowing wooden gong,
a log that cracks sharp in the ashes, and
has given wings to the charred dust.
                                  Later, it hangs
moonlike and old with woodsmoke in a black tree
up on the ridge. The crows, snared by the netted oaks,
stick still, the scraps of paper from the fire, yesterday's news
and last week's envelopes. The words come back on them
at sunrise, faintly traced. Sometimes we read
our home addresses.

THE WHITE HORSE

They guessed, as they dug off the turf,
the sign that waited for them
where the chalk lines fell out,
scattered and compact,
bones for an augury, divining stalks,
the cupped hill's ideogram: *Beast,* it said,
but do not be afraid.
This is no foreign word:
under the swell of dredging labour
it is quick and clear;
the white earth runs like water.

CORNISH WATERS

Above Boscastle

Grey, warm and stony air
hangs from the clouds in swaying pillars,
and the rain, complex, occasional,
pricks a soft skin.

The green slopes heave
down through the cloud, against the sand,
swallowed and drained off at the bay,
collapsed at journey's end.

Up on the stormy hills
the travellers drop through the grey troughs,
their breath filled up with rain,
eyes under water.

And from the sea,
the level concrete of the sea, who looks,
unmoved and private on the quay
at the land's wrecks?

St Endellion: in church

Between the twinkling granite spars,
the tide is almost at the roof,
pushing the jostling drift of beams.

Lapping insistent words in flood
cajole and smooth Atlantic scarps;
the rock grows deep around the swell.

The little waves will clap their hands,
after the rhythm drops; the stains
paint little transient peaks of dark.

Blackness of words, dense symphonies,
push at the jostling drift of beams
that seal and smooth the granite well.

Dead wood, the drift of nameless craft,
light with the memories of drowning,
hedges the fields of rhythmic dark.

The tide is turning with the roof still dry.

Goonhilly Downs

Wrapped in damp furs, the cold Sidonians
looked in the pits of tin and bought
and hammered out a tongue for awkward contracts,
laying the spiky consonants of Canaan
around the mines, the dangerous dark pools,
where wealth and death, with their loud vowels, hide.

Wedges of thorn, the spiky bone expecting
flesh that will never come, drop a black image
on to the moor's puddles, where the sky,
plain between showers, shines, a thin and equal light;
and in the mirror, the Phoenician consonants
tread back into their distant native text:

Lands before commerce, loss, desire
voiced on the thorn complaints and bargaining;
before the showers come back to dig the moor

with metal hollows mined down to the vein.
A, says the wind, and when the first rain falls,
O, says the scarred pool round its fractured spines.

Camelford (in honour of Regional Water Companies)

Rain is transparent, irresistible,
extravagant and obstinate,
it never will be wooed, to come or go,
like words, or grace.

Rain can be caught, drunk, trapped,
woven with particles of solid dark,
thickened in renal channels, flavoured
with compromising flesh.

Rain must be purchased in a thirsty time
(when knots of charity are dry to breaking point),
clouded and dense with lodging in the guts
of canny men.

Rain sours in the ruts of foresight, payment
salts it to piss, so that it cannot fall
cold on a breaking skin, graceful
for tongue and stomach.

Rain's not exhausted, can't be wooed to go;
the dark still gathers out of which,
heavy and wet as words or grace, it falls
to wash sores; flood banks.

BACH FOR THE CELLO

By mathematics we shall come to heaven.
This page the door of God's academy
for the geometer,

Where the pale lines involve a continent,
transcribe the countryside of formal light,
kindle with friction.

Passion will scorch deep in these sharp canals:
under the level moon, desire runs fast,
the flesh aches on its string,
without consummation,

Without loss.

LOS NIÑOS[1]

Niño de Vallecas

Look. Big feet and chubby legs
stretched out.
Again. The mouth, lifting a little,
knowingly. I am unhappy; I have noticed
that this is not an accident.
Again. The eyes reach vaguely.
I am unhappy. What will you do?
Are you my friend? What will you give
a child disguised
as a man dressed as a child?

Don Sebastian

What you must do is look me in the eyes
today, the eyes I turned on them, King Philip,
the Infantes, the Inquisitor, the Cardinal my master,
saying, Now, laugh; pity; befriend,
if you so dare. They looked across my head,
friendly and sorry; my ears were close enough
to hear their heaving stomachs' mirth.
So here I sit, stranger, at your eyes for once,
not at your reeking crotch. Now:
pity; befriend. I do not think
I shall be first to drop my gaze, and you may guess
what these cold knuckles hold so close.

Don Pedro

I am the little man
that potent fellows fear
for I run chuckling
between their legs
stealing the privilege of
your stuffed trunks.

Down where you do not come
there lives the world of little folk,
bright, bitter, sniggering
at your swelled dramas. Why?
down here we're hungry:
concentrates the mind.

---

[1] The sequence is prompted by Velasquez' paintings of the court dwarves of
Philip IV; from the documentary sources we know something of their histories
and character.

FIRST THING

The last bit of the dream is letters falling,
soft and regular, the papery flutter
rhythmic on the mat. Not unlike
grey tides licking sand. Waking
is water leaking in; the stuff
out there wobbles and swells
and settles grudgingly into a dryish
daytime shape. And the letters
leaking in resolve themselves
as the dry short breaths
of a nextdoor body, finding
its way out of the night
into slow breakfast time,
the food, the light, a few words,
and the apprehensive, unavoidable
opening of envelopes.

DREAM

News of another ceasefire broken: Sarajevo?
somewhere like that. Anger and shame. I stammer
to the person I am drinking with and whom I don't
know very well. I'm crying, quite a lot (I do
in dreams). We are due, next, at a seminar
on violence, held in a courthouse or a theatre,
something like that. What I remember is two speakers,
one cropped and harsh: I find it hard
to formulate my question. One bearded,
articulate and reasonable, talking of victims,
tragedy, the pathos of God trapped in a world
of risks. He sounds like dense stringed music.
It is time to leave, and I fall into step
with him or someone from the benches opposite
(theatre? chapel? parliament?), bearded,
articulate and friendly. We have much in common.
He leads me round behind the theatre
or courthouse; the path narrows between iron railings.
He rounds a corner. There is no one. Stone and iron
closing in. In front of me, a haze of wasps,
alive and dead, some sticking in the dense
and whiteish webbing stuck across the path. I feel
my legs slow down; I know there is no corner
left to turn. I feel the first sting on my right hand
between wrist and thumb. I know I am going to die.

FEOFAN GREK: THE NOVGOROD FRESCOES

Did Yeats mean this?[1] because when sages
stand in the fire, this happens. Skin
umbers and cracks and shines. And then
on hands, shoulders and skirts, the splash
and dribble; you could think the bells
have melted from their perch,
so that the roaring hollows fall, lazy as snow,
bright liquid pebbles. And then, long
after the eyes have gone, the cheekbones
gleam, razored with little scars in parallel,
the surgery of initiation, letting through
furnaces under the dun hard skin.
We slow down more and more as the heat rises; surfaces
dry up, something inside swells painfully.
The razor makes its first cut. From the oven walls,
out of the searing dusk, they smile
(not at us) blindly.

---

[1] In his poem 'Sailin g to Byzantium'. Feofan Grek's frescoes of 1378 are in the
Cathedral of the Transfiguration in the ancient city of Novgorod, a hundred
miles south of St Petersburg.

Bright post-examination weather; in the redundant
classroom, the only point seems here, the belly
of Kentucky heat, the shaven sweating mariners
singing Gregorian shanties in a slow
light evening. What do I want? What sixteen-year-olds want,
no doubt; but also: to learn how to sail that sweaty ship,
words falling moistly from the timber, shining,
Latin, American, French. And the horizon that you think
(so slow the light, so slow the gestures and the voices)
night never quite closes on.

            The same month
you made a landfall, emptied on to the shore,
gasping and heaving against a new hard element,
against the solid sand. And now I read you, years on,
leap and flail, mouth wide, reaching – you once-fluent fellow –
for the words to fix it, finding in the unfixable
a bizarre homeliness. You spent my sixteenth birthday
making a clean(ish) breast of things to the steel smile
of Abbot James. You staged show after show
for friends, then cancelled. Not to make sense is
what most matters.

            What was I seeing,
then, that summer? light from a dead star?
Not quite. But who could tell the night, closing its mouth,
the hard sand, were, after all, where the hot songs
would lead? Practise the Gothic scales for long enough

---

[1] At this time Merton, the radical monastic genius, poet and social
critic, was entangled in a tormenting and unconsummated love affair.

and they will conjure, surprisingly, this place, flat concrete blocks,
convenience foods, an empty page to look into,
finding the anger; painting, then blotting faces you might wear,
hers, yours, that only in fiction would stand still.
Not to make sense. inside the keel of sweating ribs,
not to make sense but room.

WALSINGHAM: THE HOLY HOUSE

Red kites against a dark blue sky: the flames
beating and clapping round their poise, they fight
wordlessly to hold upright against the draught.

The fat nightlights grow steep, briefly
narrowing their upended eyes, the wavering lines
converge, drop like a plumb, and for a moment

Breath sits upright against the draught, the fat flesh
caught where the beams cross, soundless, perhaps
frightened: fast, without strain, the fire stoops.

PENRHYS[1]

The ground falls sharply; into the broken glass,
into the wasted mines, and turds are floating
in the well. Refuse.

May; but the wet, slapping wind is native here,
not fond of holidays. A dour council cleaner,
it lifts discarded

Cartons and condoms and a few stray sheets
of newspaper that the wind sticks
across his face –

The worn sub-Gothic infant, hanging awkwardly
around, glued to a thin mother.
Angelus Novus:

Backing into the granite future, wings spread,
head shaking at the recorded day,
no, he says, refuse,

Not here. Still, the wind drops sharply.
Thin teenage mothers by the bus stop
shake wet hair,

Light cigarettes. One day my bus will come, says one;
they laugh. More use 'n a bloody prince,
says someone else.

---

[1] Penrhys is a council estate in the Rhondda Valley, and also (lilce
Walsingham) the site of a medieval shrine of Our Lady.

The news slips to the ground, the stone dries off,
smoke and steam drift uphill
and tentatively

Finger the leisure centre's tense walls and stairs.
The babies cry under the sun,
they and the thin girls

Comparing notes, silently, on shared
unwritten stories of the bloody stubbornness
of getting someone born.

Not iron but glass; smoother, bewildering.
We couldn't understand why they
would shake their heads and shrug,
not understanding, when they looked so near.

And not a curtain but a dome:
rays from a reasonable sun drawn in,
bent into thick and beaming probes, to drive
rational passions deep into the soil,
where the roots swelled, grew muscular
grew dense and anxious in the dark,
began to feel out for a grip to choke
each other, sent up damp and glaring shoots.

Inexorable soft pressures crack the glass.
Cold; other sounds; then piece by piece,
the shards drop a sky's worth of reasonable light
slicing the crowded greenery.

Who knows where the sky's needles go,
whose flesh is cut? But the ground dries,
under the sun, and the fat roots grow spindly
as old limbs do when there's no more blood to spare.

The devil, said the witches, had an iron prick,
icecold and smooth. Glass into iron; a reasonable sun,
nourishing, resolving, folds into a shaft
of rapists' surgery, till there's no more blood to spare.

So much, we say, for warm and clear illusion,
for the sealed surfaces of thought that incubate
the vegetable nightmares, fright, despair.
Now they can hear the music of our ironies.

Only: now we can hear, wishing
we couldn't understand, they look so near.

Physics gets nervous sometimes: can we manage?
can we keep upright on the narrow board of law
in a tight corner with the speed rising?
– so sets itself these adolescent dares: go on,
solve this! Jump; walk the wire; dodge
the zigzagging traffic. Push unlikely bundles
down canals too tight for them, spring them
from world to world, water to air,
and catch them as they drop. Tighten the passageways
so that the pitch goes razor-sharp, and the flow bumps
over more stones along the jostled path
and sounds come thicker. Squeeze, stretch,
strike; and the equations, sweating, give their answers.
Turn up the heat and choke the roads: come
to the edge of things and sounds, and look!
says physics, I can do it, I can jump and land,
and leave a map vibrating in the cloud, I move
so fast you must stand still.
                              The mica
shines in the rock as though the spray
has petrified. Physics relaxes as the stone
and water drop to the levels where the idle crocodiles
wait for what physics sends them in crushed parcels
down the chute. The test is passed, the lung
forced open; something has crossed the plaited
crossfire currents to hang steadily in the rapid air
as if said, as if written, once for all.

KAMPALA: THE EL SHADDAI COFFEE BAR

The patron sometimes calls in for a glass,
perhaps; sits with his back
to the door.

Eyes shine and water in the woodsmoke;
who can tell who might be
welcome here?

WOODWIND: KANUGA IN MARCH

Rain shades in the pines, with steady strokes
and nothing moves. The window is a screen
of drizzling verticals, normality, events,
gameshows and costume drama to be resumed
soonish. On the one tree, the patch of earth red
worries, though; alive? Ready to jump or fly? No. Watch.
Nothing moves. The bloody elbow of a branch
recording some unmanageable load of last month's
snow, a secret life exposed, spicy and naked: life,
but not as we know it, Jim? Ready to move?
the fleshy ochre timber squeezing
into a bird-shaped pellet, climbing the drizzling rods,
it lays a red trail into the wet, grows wooden wings,
hoots like an oboe as the air rushes through
a splintered mouth, moans with the recollection
of the weight that broke it into life,
ready to spring. The air smoothes its grain,
the rain points and polishes its blind head,
slowly soaks it through. The other birds watch carefully.
The moment comes when it stands still, starts falling,
drops fast with the rain, wings folded, and the steady note
climbs into the white, and the claws like a hawk
fall on the gap again at the branch's wounded corner.
The glow returns against the rain, quietly. There is, after all,
no other place to live but on the corner where the cold loads fall.
The cooing instrument rises in panic, squawks and shrills and finds
nothing to say. This is a place where, as the rain suggests,
things come home to roost. Although the red eye, the secret flesh,
won't close. I move. Have I seen anything? It winks and preens.
What do we know?

Remembering Jerusalem

JERUSALEM LIMESTONE

I
When you try
to cultivate a plot by the Dead Sea,
you find that pouring on fresh water
brings the salt
nearer the surface.

Up on the hills,
the lurching terraces are full of vines
and olives, and the terraces are rimmed
with stone, white
as a scrubbed doorstep,

White as the scurf
meandering the length of a cold shore
after polluted tides, as if the oil
and wine drained
down at last

Into a thirst
of sand and sea-water, a mouth
at the far edge of words or breath, a face
with salt
breaking the surface.

II
And when you see
the staircase hills, white, olive, grey,
the stones hang there like snow
along the edge
of evergreens.

The vines and groves
are posies, stuck by children's hands
into the winter soil, hard
under blankets;
tomorrow dead.

Winter's what lasts.
The oil glow sinking like bonfires
into grey flakes, a twisted log
or two, already
slipping down

Under tonight's
fresh fall; only the cold
can be relied on to come back.
The wine is chilled
long before harvest.

III
When you touch,
your hands will come away dry,
faintly powdered, classroom hands, to rub
back into damp
adhesive life

Up on the hills
the lurching lines cover the board
we can't decode. This is a country
thick with scripts
most won't know.

But the dust
sits in the folds of clothes
and lungs and larynx. What we want
to say explodes
a chalky retching.

Winter.
The dusty coughs like guns,
The class dismissed, untaught.
Something not understood.
The white dry hill.

GETHSEMANE

Who said that trees grow easily
compared with us? What if the bright
bare load that pushes down on them
insisted that they spread and bowed
and pleated back on themselves and cracked
and hunched? Light dropping like a palm
levelling the ground, backwards and forwards?

Across the valley are the other witnesses
of two millennia, the broad stones
packed by the hand of God, bristling
with little messages to fill the cracks.
As the light falls and flattens what grows
on these hills, the fault lines dart and spread,
there is room to say something, quick and tight.

Into the trees' clefts, then, do we push
our folded words, thick as thumbs?
somewhere inside the ancient bark, a voice
has been before us, pushed the densest word
of all, abba, and left it to be collected by
whoever happens to be passing, bent down
the same way by the hot unreadable palms.

CALVARY

The metalled O. Like Bethlehem, like
a baroque drain in the marble floor;
when your hand has been sucked in, it comes away
from its complicity moist,
grimy, sweet-scented.

THE STONE OF ANOINTING

All day they oil and polish, rubbing
as if the stone were troubled, rippled with
the angel's windy touch; as if the stone
were sprung like a cramped muscle, and a hard warm hand
could loosen it; as if the hoarse determined breath
and the hot oil could stop the choking, break a seal
on some unseen and frozen lung.
As if they couldn't see themselves. And only when
the stone falls still will their tired polished
faces look back at them; ready to receive
Christ laid on them like a cloth.

EASTER EVE: SEPULCHRE

Constantine knew, of course, just what he wanted:
smooth verticals and marble, crushed glass rolled underfoot,
room for archangels with their orbs and wands,
space for cool power to stroll, relaxed and heavy-footed

Out to the little scented hedges, under a cross that shimmers,
silver and rubies, soft shadows lapping at the ankles.
He cut and smoothed, levelled and piled and spread:
light; crystal; breezy veils; a new, enlightened holy hill.

History (or something) disagreed. The centuries squared up,
exchanged curt, recognizing nods, moved in,
folded and packed, crumpled and stripped and boxed:
the shadows shook themselves, lurched up and smiled

From a new height; people found other things
to do with silver. Air from the marble lungs
is punched out, and the colonnades are crushed and processed
into a maze of ditches, damp stone capsules,

Whorls, cavities, corners with don't-ask smells
and fairground decoration. A collapsing star, screwing its stuff
into the dark: soaring heat, density, a funnel
spinning towards the opposite of anything.

*

Saturday afternoon, the bodies squashed, wet, boxed,
breathing into the shadows full of smells and tinsel;
flame leaks and spits out of the singularity,
sparks a cracked bell. Iron, rope, smoke

Pant in the tight dark, a light-footed,
high-strung passing. Afterwards we breathe,
dry off the sweat and crying, ask what history
is after, bullying us into waking, into this oppositeness.

LOW SUNDAY: ABU GHOSH

Calm, fluent, the Mass moves
like robes on a walking body, upright
and in no hurry, the chanted French
swings loose between the stresses.

Finding its way in here
something not quite the hard dawn,
crackling out of the grave, but
heavy, lumbering maybe, quiet,

As it pads in from downstairs,
lies down and looks at us, something
idle (maybe), breathing just audibly,
not without noticing; not to be avoided.

Graves and Gates

'... that through the grave and gate of death we may pass to our joyful resurrection'
BOOK OF COMMON PRAYER

RILKE'S LAST ELEGY

Die ewige Strömung
reisse durch beide Bereiche alle Alter
immer mit sich und übertönt sie in beiden.

The river flows in both kingdoms. On the side
we don't see, the moon side, it collects the things
we don't see: slivers of ice between the ripples,
and small blue leprosies, and tiny stars that prick
and cut us as we drink; moon-sounds, the anxious hawking
of a fox, the little screams of casual prey, the car-alarm
five silent streets away (you know that if you wake
and look, you'll never find it; it is another kingdom).

So when you whisper into the stream, the words run
round through the moon's valleys, where we don't see,
coming back strange: swollen or scarred, not lining up
and answering. This time round, they prick and scratch
the throat till it flows black, a winter river
fed by the rains we don't see. Bit by bit
the other kingdom spreads, and what we say drowns softly
all sounds smothered. Then the river dries. The earth

Puckers and shrinks, as quiet as the moon. And a few words
lie in their white bed, covenanting stones.

NIETZSCHE: TWILIGHT

At the clinic, he broke windows, shouting
that there were guns behind them, desperate
not to be shielded by the thin, deceiving skin
that looked as if it wasn't there. He liked
the opaque curtain or the open sky; not this.
His mother took him home; out for walks,
she told him, Put on your nice professor's face,
when they met friends. His head grew vast,
pulling him downwards till he could not breathe.
At night he roared; during the day, My voice
is not nice, he would whisper. White,
swollen, his skull drowned him like a stone,
his breath, at the end, the sound
of footsteps on broken glass.

SIMONE WEIL AT ASHFORD

Upstairs into the air: a young god,
pupils dilated, blows into his little flute.
At each stair's end, he breaks it, reaches for a new one,
climbs again. Below the crowd blurs, hums,
ahead the sky is even, dark from the bare sun.
Breaking the last instrument, he waits,
and in a while they will tear out his heart,
now it is still and simple as the rise and fall
of tides. The crowd and the sun breathe him in.

No, we don't walk like him. We stagger up
the steps in padded jackets, moonboots,
crash-helmets, filters and shades. In gravity.
Some of us try to strip; but what's beneath is
very cold, even under the dark bare sun:
a stiff, gaunt crying, I must not be loved,
and I must not be seen, and if I cannot walk like god,
at least I can be light and hungry, hollowing my guts
till I'm a bone the sentenced god can whistle through.

TOLSTOY AT ASTAPOVO[1]

Off through the looking-glass he ran:
into the world of hedges, brooks, black and white
    cantonments,
the snapping Queen to urge him on, the fevers
rising and falling, painting black or white
the country of his choices. All around the iron lines
run to a point. Ahead of him strolls Platon,
not looking back; he runs till he is breathless,
burning, but he can't catch him. In the next-door squares
the pieces crowd, the journalists, the relatives, the hopefuls,
the *starets* in the ladies' loo, the script consultants,
newsreel men, police. Check.

Heat and smoke in the little squares; shivering,
he thinks of taking up a long-lost country skill
as quaint as thatching, complicated, unselfconscious,
the sort of thing you pick up in the hours
of glazed winter boredom, the absent-minded endlessness
of a poor childhood. *How do peasants die?*
Some things you can't get into at this age. He knew
he was too old to die, fingers too stiff for plaiting
the spiny ends. He put his head down in the straw.
Mate. All the words came tumbling
backwards out of his dream.

---

[1] Leo Tolstoy died in the stationmaster's house (now a museum) in Astapovo (now
Tolstoy).

BEREAVEMENTS

In memory of Jim and Letty Morgan

Beginning with the purchase order:
notice was served on some years' livelihood
(no choice: lucid imperatives drive rapidly;
 they need their motorways), and then
the hospital, and notice served on some years' love
(or something like it), confident highspeed
mortality (no choice, not even purchase)
So that he watched the dusty rubbled bed,
those months, the engines ploughing up
                              some years of him,
the furrows slowly merging in the flesh and mud,
the shrinking face, the swelling pools, bewildered,
waiting for clearance. Till the knot was tied,
black gravel rollered down, where the imperatives
run smoothly off for the horizon. In the house,
behind the window she put in out back, he sits
and sees remembered grass still springing underneath
the lucid wheels. He will not go,
not leave the stranded house; his livelihood,
his years, are razored down to this,
                              eyes at this window.
Nowhere else, no choice.

WINTERREISE: FOR GILLIAN ROSE, 9 DECEMBER 1995

Morning

The flat fields tramp towards the Severn.
I know there is no cliff to drop from
at their edge, only the sand and the wet still sheets.

This morning, though, the thick and chest-constricting
light, the level, rose-grey clouds and the remains
of icy fog stand between fields and water,

And the horizon has to be a steep edge, has to be
the cliff where Gloucester fell that never-to-be measured
drop from his body to the ground.
And down, a long way down, below the frost,
must be soft embers sending up the light
from fires the night-fog has muffled but not killed.

Afternoon

Still, where you were concerned, we always
arrived too late; too late, myopic, short of sleep,
with fingers stumbling to decipher messages
you left for us, engraved in a hard surface.
It was a distant relative of yours who drove
his lawyer's reed into the black Sinai basalt
till the calligraphy of little streams broke out
to age the hopeless rock as if with history,
as if with words; another kinsman, distant or not too distant,
writing in falling sweat on stone, body to ground, something
his friends never quite managed to read. Tracing, unthinkingly,
a pattern of spilled wine on the dayroom table,
never quite managing to meet each other's eyes, or not for long,

we test the feel of an unyielding difficulty, not yet sure
of handling this, of finding where the streams combine,
reading what the wet fingertips decode.

Night

Dying by degrees, perhaps, is a winter journey:
connections cancelled unexplained, the staff,
their patience ebbing, closing amenities, one by one, around you.

The temperature falls, and for an hour you sit
on a plastic bench, aching for sleep,
under the surly light that strips you

For some always-delayed inspection; so even,
so hard, that for so long you cannot see the dark:
the homely dark, with its fierce small fires.

FLIGHT PATH
For Delphine Williams; August 1999

Dead souls walk straight as Roman legions
from Bredon Hill, striding from fort to fort,
from one sullen, round-shouldered rise
to the next, stopping (perhaps) on each to gape
and swallow and exchange dumb looks, and wait for orders.

The track runs through the solid tribal world:
crosses a motorway at thirty-seven degrees, lays
a cold strip across a sheep's back, slips
between cup and lip, between eye and screen, between
my child's hand and my own, eases between the window and the wind.

The Roman road ignores the aboriginals, their maps
and calendars. But we shuffling primitives can't fail to see
this is the occupying power. Sooner or later, we shall have to learn
to shape our mouths, measure our stride like theirs,
and look nowhere but to the next grazed, wind-scrubbed summit.

CEIBWR: CLIFFS

For Aneurin Williams; September 1999

The quilt of willowherb muffles
the stream before it drops
invisible to the beach;
the moist whisper thinned
in its straight seaward fall,
the shore sound coming back up, dry
as two palms rubbing steadily
close to your ear, or pages
fingered through, or a hand
stroking an unshaved cheek, hard;
or a thick old fabric, tearing
very slowly. Sea on stone
never settles for good if this
is a story of meeting or
an endless creeping scission:
a palmer's kiss, book skimmed
for the familiar quote, touching
the distant face against
hospital pillows, or
slow surgery, faded cloth
pulled and surrendering
every breath unstitching
something. Whatever,
the hoarse bass echo
doesn't change: just the one
voice, touching or tearing.

WINDSOR ROAD CHAPEL

Cinema (Odeon or Capitol) circa 1959:
only no curtains, just an even, tight-pinned bedsheet
of timber, and a blunt, empty cockpit.
Nothing, it says, will come over your shoulder,
no hidden reels, throwing a hazy line

Across the smoke to play the rainbow fish
that slip around, behind, our watered eyes.
This is the board for unexpected news,
a death, a resignation, raw, cold
as the air outside, flat as the turned-down wish.

God, it seems doesn't live in water, glimpse and flash,
mirror and shade, not still until the day's
damp end. The message on the wires
rubs at the skin's impatient folds
in dry, pale itches, drifts of my neighbour's ash.

The most familiar artefact of brass and pine
nags at the memory; you know what's going to fit
the timber cabinet before too long, the drought
that cures the flesh and seals the blood.
Board: gate: departure, says the sign.

Off you go, then, on static-laden floors,
drawn – as we all are – by unwelcome news;
but even now, not able not to pause
and listen for pursuing streams, rolled
shining and stuttering downhill to the exit doors.

DEATHSHIP
in memory of R.S. Thomas

The last years, words from a window
smoothing the sea, the iron back and forth
to probe the fugitive wrinkles
carving a path down to the lost gate.

What hid in the pale clefts till now
feels for the light, a soft uncertain
fingering as if through
stone, through furrows of flint.

The tides pressed neat as for an evening out:
time to drag down a black boat from the shed,
off through the gate, to balance
on the slow sea at dark, ready to sail.

The smoke will rise, the cloudy pillar
wavering across the sky's long page.
At dawn, somewhere westward,
the boat flares in a blaze of crying birds.

Celtia

GUNDESTRUP: THE HORNED GOD

You know him. Sitting and sitting,
sitting until the moss grows
over his eyes, until

The stark bone branches
burst through his skull, until
his mouth and hand and gut will

Shape the one round, tense
metal syllable, at which
the beasts stand still

Snouts cocked and hairs on end,
the salmon frozen in mid-leap,
gripped by the unexpected rider's will.

Sit: till you grow hollow,
round as a cauldron, and your mouth
holds the world cocked, dumb and chill,

And from your brow the knitting bones
twist to a forest of hard sounds; among them things
stand still and frightened. Well

You know.

THE SKY FALLING

*'They [the Celtic chiefs] told him that they feared only one thing, that
the sky should fall'*
Arrian, *The Expedition of Alexander*

A joke, perhaps? They still
do it, solemnly meeting
the earnest foreigner's enquiry.
Because there could have been,
surely, no terror

For the lime-rinsed and technicolour –
shirted, head-hungry, henpecked
louts who so irritated
dry Caesar in the promise of an end
so brisk and flat

And messy, like flies squashed
between the pages as the book
claps shut; dying of the applause
of heaven and earth when they
join hands

At the show's end. Or maybe,
after all, serious. Think of them
lurching out of the doorway
to breathe, pee, vomit,
packed with booze

Kebabs and mutual admiration,
into the cold; the snow just starting
and the sky slips gently
and piecemeal into the grass
and vanishes,

Fragments of brief intricacy,
like the bard's lovely, hot,
cosseting songs indoors,
the words that freeze great doings
(rapes, wars)

In symmetries and stars; and going
nowhere. The stories sink
into the grass at night,
and the earth sits there,
not applauding,

Spreading an empty palm;
swallowing the sparks of damp
and formal brilliance. Very
quiet.
No joke.

POSIDONIUS AND THE DRUID

Ridges of bone, moulded, you'd think, by awkward thumbs,
freckles, red stubble, and the large pale astigmatic eyes;
the voice hoarse, fluent, not deep.
Well. People come, like you, he says, looking for secrets.
What we learned from Pythagoras. For a consoling echo
of your sweet doctrine from the untouched caves
of us poor primitives. (Leaning to me.) Do you like
what I've to show you? On his open hand
a knife, bone-handled, stained and smooth.
Your logos is a child, he says, chattering to itself
while it plays on the sand. I am a swimmer.
I am a salmon and a seal. My streams
are made of many fluids, dark swaying planes
on which I travel still as sleep; or where
I leap like silver. The sea. Rain on the skin,
and sweat. Tears and the river over stones.
My blood and yours: the tide that beats below the skin
or in the pulsing from the severed vein,
or from my organ, or from yours, or else the urine
from the hanged man, jerking among the leaves,
whose motions speak to me. Over these waves
I learn to skim my hands, and in these wells
my tongue explores, drinks words.

                              I take the knife;
like rubbing fingers on a worn inscription,
read it. In my mind, briefly: flat plains,
a straight road running to the edge of things, drab
unfamiliar carts packed close with silent people,
knowing and not knowing what this journey is
on which they're sent by blood and wisdom and

dark quiet waters, and I reach out breathless for the shore,
children and sand, the noise and the unsafety,
drift, spars and groundlessness, but still the anchorage
proper to talking beings.

ALTAR TO THE MOTHERS

Soft-cheeked and honey-breasted,
fruit tumbling at their feet like children, and
semantically-loaded sheaves of corn,
beautiful, terrible; warm thighs and mysteries
and a calm dark regard out of their timeless eyes...

Actually no (if this is really them):
they stand in solid sexless line,
headscarved and overcoated, waiting for a bus
to Ebbw Vale or Rotherham; bleak damp endurance of
the never-up-to-standard world.

Men (rightly) shivering laid oil and wine
and sacrificed new shoes, pubertal hair,
unsatisfactory girlfriends, self-respect,
nodding in desperation at the granite words
you can't switch off. No, you do what *you* want, love,

Don't think of me. We've always done what seemed the right thing
for you, pet. If you don't respect
yourself, no-one will do it for you. If you've got
your health, there's nothing you can't cope with. What time
do you call this? Why aren't you eating?

You do what you want, love. Divinity is manifest
in the sublime command, Ignore this order; making sure
that you won't, ever. Refused, victorious, inexpugnable,
they settle back, having secured that there will never be
an up-to-standard offering, a world

Free to leave home, to call time what we like.

EXPERIENCING DEATH

Don't know a thing about this trip we're going on; they don't
give much away about it. So we don't know where to stand
to look at the unwelcome destination, how to see our death.
Amazed? entranced? or loathing? How the tragic mask twists things

Out of an honest shape! But still, the world can give
you quite a cast-list to choose from. Just don't
forget; as long as it's the audience's reaction
that worries you, death's at your elbow on the boards.

No audience fancies corpses. Only when *you* went offstage,
the flats you slipped through let in something else,
a streak of truth: the colour of real foliage
under real sunshine in a real woodland.

For us, the show must go on. All those lines
we learned, struggling and panicky, the stagey gestures
ordered by some director we can't put a face to... and then you,
struck off the list, you who are real now a long way off,

Your far-off thereness sometimes overtakes us still, falling
around us like that streak of daylight green, and then
we find, just for a bit, we can play life, not scripts;
not give a damn about applause.

Rilke

ROUNDABOUT, JARDIN DU LUXEMBOURG

Out of that foreign land, the gaudy horses
bounce with conviction for a while (never mind
the shadows from the canopy) – the foreign land
that hangs around long enough after closing time before it fades.

They all look feisty enough, even the ones
(quite a few) with carts hitched on. Oh look!
A big bad lion seems to have got in. Oh look!
A sweet baby white elephant. What next?

Oh look! A stag, just like the ones you see
out in the woods, except of course this one
happens to have a little girl in blue
strapped in a saddle,

                      and the big bad lion's
carrying a little boy in white, who's hanging on
for dear life, while the lion grins and slobbers –
Look! the sweet baby white elephant again...
Those girls are getting too big for the ride,
but there they go, giggling and darting sparky looks
all over the place in mid-flight, and they – oh,
there's the sweet
                baby
                    white...

Round and round and round and round and round.
Red. Green. Grey. Red. Aching to stop.
Nowhere to go. The little profiles sketchy, hardly started.
Listen! There's someone laughing as they spin,
as if they were – well, happy, blissful even;
wasting their breath, casting a shimmer round
this blind asthmatic game.

Rilke

ANGEL

He bends his head away, says his hard No to everything
that might commit him, tie him down,
because there's always something circling, always
just about to land, something enormous
pushing up through his heart.

                And the deep blackness
of the sky is full, for him, of shapes,
and any one of them could summon him – come here!
see this! So for God's sake, don't try to put
what weighs *you* down into those airy hands of his;
because it's you they'd grab for.

                In the middle of the night
they'd burrow in and scrabble like a maniac
round your house, and clutch you, wrestle you to the floor,
squeezing and kneading, wanting to sculpt and hollow,
to push you, break you out of the form you know
that clothes you round.

HYMN FOR THE MERCY SEAT

Wonder is what the angels' eyes hold, wonder:
The eyes of faith, too, unbelieving in the strangeness,
Looking on him who makes all being gift,
Whose overflowing holds, sustains,
Who sets what is in shape,
Here in the cradle, swaddled, homeless,
And here adored by the bright eyes of angels,
The great Lord recognised.

Sinai ablaze, the black pall rising,
Through it the horn's pitch, high, intolerable,
And I, I step across the mortal frontier
Into the feast, safe in my Christ from slaughter.
Beyond that boundary all loss is mended,
The wilderness is filled, for he,
Broker between the litigants, stands in the breach,
Offers himself for peace.

Between the butchered thieves, the mercy seat, the healing,
The place for him to test death's costs,
Who powers his very killers' arms,
Drives in the nails that hold him, while he pays
The debt of brands torn from the bonfire,
Dues to his Father's law, the flames of justice
Bright for forgiveness now, administering
Liberty's contract.

Soul, look. This is the place where all kings' monarch
Rested a corpse, the maker of our rest, and in
His stillness all things always move,
Within his buried silence.

Song for the lost, and life; wonder
For angels' straining eyes, God's flesh.
They praise together, they adore,
'To him', they shout, 'only to him'.

And I, while there is breath left to me,
Say, Thanksgiving, with a hundred thousand words,
Thanksgiving: that there is a God to worship,
There is an everlasting matter for my singing;
Who with the worst of us, in what
He shares with me, cried under tempting,
A child and powerless, the boundless
Living true God,

Flesh rots: instead, aflame, along with heaven's singers,
I shall pierce through the veil, into the land
Of infinite astonishment, the land
Of what was done at Calvary;
I shall look on what never can be seen, and still
Shall live, look on the one who died and who still lives
And shall; look in eternal jointure and communion,
Not to be parted.

I shall lift up the name that God
Sets out to be a mercy seat, a healing, and the veils,
And the imaginings and shrouds have gone, because
My soul stands now, his finished likeness,
Admitted now to share his secret, that his blood and hurt
Showed once, now I shall kiss the Son
And never turn away again. And never
Turn away.

From the Welsh of Ann Griffiths

I SAW HIM STANDING

Under the dark trees, there he stands,
there he stands; shall he not draw my eyes?
I thought I knew a little
how he compels, beyond all things, but now
he stands there in the shadows. It will be
Oh, such a daybreak, such bright morning,
when I shall wake to see him
as he is.

He is called Rose of Sharon, for his skin
is clear, his skin is flushed with blood,
his body lovely and exact; how he compels
beyond ten thousand rivals. There he stands,
my friend, the friend of guilt and helplessness,
to steer my hollow body
over the sea.

The earth is full of masks and fetishes,
what is there here for me? are these like him?
Keep company with him and you will know:
no kin, no likeness to those empty eyes.
He is a stranger to them all, great Jesus.
What is there here for me? I know
what I have longed for. Him to hold
me always.

From the Welsh of Ann Griffiths

STRATA FLORIDA

Wind murmurs in the trees at Ystrad Fflur
but does not wake
the dozen abbots dozing in their tombs
while the leaves shake.

Dead with his clever verses, Dafydd too
lies in his bed
Among forgotten warlords, swords dulled,
armour shed.

Summer will come and rouse the wind-stripped trees.
But not the men.
Stones unobtrusively decay. They will not
stand again.

Defeat, oblivion, rotting monuments
of dead belief.
Why is it then I find no words, here, quietly,
for private grief?

From the Welsh of T. Gwynn Jones

SONG FOR A BOMB

I split and scatter him who splits and scatters,
And in my falling there is Adam's Fall.
Where in this vacuum will you find purpose,
Where is the pattern where a purpose dwells?

It only takes the naked brain to think me,
It only takes a human hand to shape,
And youthful nimbleness to bring to action.
What are you waiting for? Create.

My master quietly pursues his business,
Patient untying of the knotted heart.
Till, fearfully and wonderfully crafted,
Last of his servants forth I come to wait.

My master is the worm that gnaws the root,
My master is the canker in the tree.
But I shall tidy him away for ever
On to the bonfire of death's ecstasy.

From the Welsh of Waldo Williams

IN THE DAYS OF CAESAR

In the days of Caesar, when his subjects went to be reckoned,
there was a poem made, too dark for him (naive with power)
    to read.
It was a bunch of shepherds who discovered
in Bethlehem of Judah, the great music beyond reason and
    reckoning:
shepherds, the sort of folk who leave the ninety-nine behind
so as to bring the stray back home, they heard it clear,
the subtle assonances of the day, dawning toward cock-crow,
the birthday of the Lamb of God, shepherd of mortals.

Well, little people, and my little nation, can you see
the secret buried in you, that no Caesar ever captures in his
    lists?
Will not the shepherd come to fetch us in our desert,
gathering us in to give us birth again, weaving us into one
in a song heard in the sky over Bethlehem?
He seeks us out as wordhoard for his workmanship, the
    laureate of heaven

From the Welsh of Waldo Williams

AFTER SILENT CENTURIES
For the Catholic martyrs of Wales

The centuries of silence gone, now let me weave a celebration;
Because the heart of faith is one, the moment glows in which
Souls recognise each other, one with the great tree's kernel at
    the root of things.

They are at one with the light, where peace masses and gathers
In the infinities above my head; and where the sky moves into
    the night,
Then each one is a spyhole for my darkened eyes, lifting the veil.

John Roberts, Trawsfynydd: a pauper's priest,
Breaking bread for the journey when the plague weighed on
    them,
Knowing the power of darkness on its way to break, crumble,
    his flesh.

John Owen, carpenter: so many hiding places
Made by his tireless hands for old communion's sake,
So that the joists are not undone, the beam pulled from the roof.

Richard Gwyn: smiling at what he saw in their faces, said,
'I've only sixpence for your fine' – pleading his Master's case,
His charges (for his life) were cheap as that.

Oh, they ran swift and light. How can we weigh them,
    measure them,
The muster of their troops, looking down into damnation?
Nothing, I know, can scatter those bound by the paying of one
    price,

The final silent tariff. World given in exchange for world,
The far frontiers of agony to buy the Spirit's leadership,
The flower paid over for the root, the dying grain to be his cradle.

Their guts wrenched out after the trip to torment on the hurdle,
And before the last gasp when the ladder stood in front of them
For the souls to mount, up to the wide tomorrow of their dear
    Lord's Golgotha.

You'd have to tell a tale of them, a great, a memorable tale,
If only, Welshmen, you were, after all, a people.

From the Welsh of Waldo Williams

DIE BIBELFORSCHER
For the Protestant martyrs of the Third Reich

Earth is a hard text to read; but the king
has put his message in our hands, for us to carry
sweating, whether the trumpets of his court
sound near or far. So for these men:
they were the bearers of the royal writ,
clinging to it through spite and hurts and wounding.

The earth's round fullness is not like a parable, where meaning
breaks through, a flash of lightning, in the humid, heavy dusk;
imagination will not conjure into flesh the depths
of fire and crystal sealed under castle walls of wax, but still
they kept their witness pure in Buchenwald,
pure in the crucible of hate penning them in.

They closed their eyes to doors that might have opened
if they had put their names to words of cowardice;
they took their stand, backs to the wall, face to face with
    savagery,
and died there, with their filth and piss flowing together,
arriving at the gates of heaven,
their fists still clenched on what the king had written.

Earth is a hard text to read. But what we can be certain of
is that the screaming mob is insubstantial mist;
in the clear sky, the thundering assertions fade to nothing.
There the Lamb's song is sung, and what it celebrates
is the apocalypse of a glory
pain lays bare.

From the Welsh of Waldo Williams

These two fields a green sea-shore, the tide spilling
radiance across them, and who knows
where such waters rise? And I'd had years
in a dark land, looking: where did it, where did he
come from then? Only he'd been there
all along. Who though? who
was this marksman loosing off bolts
of sudden light? One and the same the lightning
hunter across the field, the hand to tilt
and spill the sea, who from the vaults
above the bright-voiced whistlers, the keen darting plovers,
brought down on me such quiet, such

Quiet: enough to rouse me. Up to that day
nothing had worked but the hot sun to get me going,
stir up drowsy warm verses: like blossom
on gorse that crackles in the ditches, or like the army of dozy
    rushes, dreaming
of clear summer sky. But now: imagination
shakes off the night. Someone is shouting
(who?), Stand up and walk. Dance. Look.
Here is the world entire. And in the middle
of all the words, who is hiding? Like this
is how it was. There on the shores of light
between these fields, under these clouds.

Clouds: big clouds, pilgrims, refugees,
red with the evening sun of a November storm.
Down where the fields divide, and ash and maple
cluster, the wind's sound, the sound of the deep,
is an abyss of silence. So who was it stood

there in the middle of this shameless glory, who
stood holding it all? Of every witness witness,
the memory of every memory, the life
of every life? who with a quiet word
calms the red storms of self, till all
the labours of the whole wide world
fold up into this silence.

And on the silent sea-floor of these fields,
his people stroll. Somewhere between them,
through them, around them, there is a new voice
rising and spilling from its hiding place
to hold them, a new voice, call it the poet's;
as it was for some of us, the little group
who'd been all day mounting assault
against the harvest with our forks, dragging
the roof-thatch over the heavy meadow. So near,
we came so near then to each other, the quiet huntsman
spreading his net around us.
Listen! you can
just catch his whistling, hear it?

Whistling, across the centuries of blood
on the grass, and the hard light of pain; whistling
only your heart hears. Who was it then, for God's sake?
mocking our boasts, tracking our every trail and slipping past
all our recruiting sergeants? Don't you know?
says the whistling, Don't you remember?
don't you recognise? it says; until we do.
And then, our ice age over, think of the force
of hearts released, springing together, think
of the fountains breaking out, reaching up
after the sky, and falling back, showers
of falling leaves, waters of autumn.

Think every day, under the sun,
under these clouds, think every night of this,
with every cell of your mind's branching swelling shoots;
but with the quiet, the same quiet, the steady breath,
the steady gaze across the two fields, holding still
the vision: fair fields full of folk;

for it will come, dawn of his longed-for coming,
and what a dawn to long for. He will arrive, the outlaw,
the huntsman, the lost heir making good his claim
to no-man's land. The exiled king
is coming home one day; the rushes sweep aside
to let him throu gh.

From the Welsh of Waldo Williams

ANGHARAD

All night and every night, she shares her bed
with jostling anxieties, jostling celebrations;
the pains keep her awake, so do the party noises,
all of them welcomed and nursed in her heart's deep seas,
the soil round her doors churned up by the distressed,
the fragile, who know their way infallibly into her courts.
All that she does weaves her a gown to wear,
bright scarlet, running down to cover every inch.

Carrying the chaos of those so breakable hearts,
binding her strength in with theirs to face out the terrors;
the blue crystal dawn of the Kingdom's day
sits on her lap, her own bright daylight,
level and simple, pouring the hospitable wine,
wine for the King's feast, wine for the wound's sting.
Light turns towards light; searching for his clear sun,
she moulds afresh in praise the early-morning unspoilt world.
The sun's sister and the four winds' sister and the sister
for days when the waves are bitter and passionate,
and sister too of the anxious watchful star
and its insistent oversight calling us forward.

Fruits from her tree she uses to calm and mend
what anger shatters or jealousy, hands smoothing
wide, unconfined, the gift indifferent to frontiers.
And that no less frontierless ancient agony becomes
longing that tells us plainly where its roots lie
deep in the soil, deep in a black earth.
So what she gives God, she gives from earth's two faces,
the pain, the festival; the tense surprise of sound and metre knitting.
And then is what she gives to us, clear under God's sky –
The priesthood of her caring.

From the Welsh of Waldo Williams

INVOCATION: A SCULPTURE FOR WINTER
Monasterio di Bose, Northern Italy, January 2003

Landscape in pale concrete: the abstract downs,
hillocks and gullies, only adjusting slowly
into twin faces staring, cranium to cranium,
at the dove-grey, eagerly bending sky.

The first cold sting falls hours before dawn
out of the heavy miles of cloud, stirred
to an answer by the face seen only
from so far, only at night, and when

The cold has folded up the colours, shut down
wind and growing, and the rustle, crack and damp
of the short day. Sounds come sideways
like landscape at earth level, but then

They're put out for the night; we don't
have anything to go on but the sensed
profile alongside, whose eyes we can't see.
Into the fast-approaching heavy heaven

We look, guessing what open mouth brings down
the random, uninhibited and unrepeatable
designs that will pile up in these gulfs,
guessing why what we can't see draws the lick and kiss

To our strange neighbour's skull.

DEATH ROW, LUZEERA JAIL

What do they spell, the fairy lights
draping the yard outside the cells?
A daily Christmas? Unwrapping the surprises
before dawn? Another day isn't, for everyone,
something to take for granted. But by the time
the sun is up, what is there left
but sitting in the litter? The new Rolex
tells you tomorrow is already planned
(and not by you). Now wake the elders,
who have ten years seniority or twenty here
in this cramped living room; but they
won't help. They have their fill of presents.
They wink back, knowingly, from time to time
at all the little glass bulbs that won't grow
into flowers. But still: on Christmas night
all Christians sing. Guests are received with smiles
and reassured: don't worry, it isn't news
that's welcome here. You needn't tell us
anything but what we know, what the lights spell:
a guest as always, as already, here
as the damp ammoniac floor.

Luzeera Jail is the main prison in Kampala; when I visited it some of
those in the condemned section had been there for up to twenty-three
years.

MARTYRS' MEMORIAL, NAMUGONGO

The rushes by the water
We gather every day...

So, patiently, the long reeds are laid,
smoothed, dried and rolled in homely sheaves
and stacked across the beams, too high (you hope)
for sparks. Remains of light poke a splinter
here and there through into the moving eye, but this
is a skill too practised and domestic for mistakes.

So too, like a tall reed, each young neighbour,
shaking the drops of an alien river off his skin,
is gathered, wrapped in the homely thatch,
stacked carefully, sparked into a protective blaze
whose oiled smoke builds a skilful roof
over the panic and the piled drugged anger

That beats the earth, the drums, behind the king's
long curtains. Plaited fumes weave patiently
across a bare sky, and the rain keeps off,
the splinter of the sun probes and is blunted,
rolled in the tight black thatch with the needling
sounds they will make as the smoke canopy builds steeply.

Burned men, after a while, make sounds like birds,
almost too high to hear. The roof's pitch.
When the smoke has cleared, the bare light
enquires, Are you safe now? Whose house is this?
Your skill has burned your home. And the bird cries
from the bare sky say, Yes, you will live here now.
Yes, every day.

Namugongo is the site of the burning alive of some of the first
Christian converts in Uganda in 1886 at the order of King Mwanga.

The riverbed, between the road
and the railway line is dry
in summer;

Soft sand, like air or water
welcomes and at once forgets
your step.

Eyes closed, you could be walking
shallow dunes, walking the edge
of ocean;

Open your eyes, go on across
the bridge, under the peeling birch
and pine.

The swaying leaves and needles
spin light from shafts, crests,
faces, hands,

As if, under the sea, you looked up
into the lightning, into the firing
circuits above,

Where the crisp waves are catching
the sun's wild leap from plane
to plane.

The forest fingers the summer sky,
a child's stubby arm from the pram
waving

In search of nose and lips and breast,
feeling; not knowing; recognising;
feeling

Being seen. The leaping and the firing,
learning your way round a face against
the sky.

At night, Serafim knelt on the same rock
three years long, walked from the sand
into the sea,

And drowned, night after night,
when the sun did not dance,
or the trees

Caress, and like a bear he rubbed
and nuzzled into the dark, blind
and appalled

And hungry, until the rock began
to smell of honey. Quickly he made
for the surface,

Breathed, was blinded again by the first
dry lined leaf falling from the birch,
the first

Dry lined face falling from the forgotten
worlds of sand and hurt, of death
and shining drought.

In the barrel of your lungs,
Father, the hammer swung for the first
leaping blow

Of Paschal Matins, fingers closing
like a child's on the found flesh.
My joy. My joy.

THE NIGHT KITCHEN: DREAMWORK

1.   *Drawing the Curtains*

The stage set beckons, a crooked street where dark falls,
and the windows angle, wall-eyed, from each other; my face
handed aslant, mirror to mirror, my voice in ricochet,
re-dressed: a low-budget chorus, recycled, rethreaded,
breathlessly changing costumes in the wings.

Cords break: too much to hold. Curtain. No curtain calls,
and afterwards the deep muffled seats, the velvet pillows,
where, with the lights up suddenly, nothing stirs.
I turn my head. You never meet another soul
in these parts. The scattered things

Under the stalls or by the exits are what got dropped
last time. Time after time I buy my ticket,
hungry, erect, shaking, to see what happens when
I dress up as my enemies or God or Mum and Dad,
touching the spiny small things daylight doesn't let me see

That lodge, casual, in nails and skin. When the day has stopped,
lights out, the real work starts; listening for cavities
inside the walls, squinting after the freezing grief trapped in between
those doubled glassy wings, straining to catch
myself saying a stranger's shattering words to me.

2..   *Gallery: Impressionists*

All through the day, the currents whisk up
sluggish pigments, tiny crests, inverted
whirlpools that end with a glossy wet flick
into bottomless air. As turbulence
drops with the sun, I close my eyes
and back away, don't open them until
my back's against the wall. And there
they are, those sticky twirls of oil,
sucked by the roving vacuums of the mind
in tousled protest, there they are, composed
in lakes and lilies, harvests, triumphant tympanums,
foggy implacable rivers under the window.

3.   *Incubus*

In your light, said someone,
we shall see light; and in my dark,
dark? Digging, silent, uninterrupted,

Through the strata, why stop? I know
the next one or the next is terror.
the next is always terror.

I am what I cannot bear. Why stop?
I know the face below the face below
the face is what I cannot push off, push out, bear.

4.   *The Place*

Yes; but also the place that has been
waiting. When the corner is turned,
there is a slope down to the bay,
in heavy shadow.

Waiting. There is a low house
of sharp stones with rugs inside
and little cold windows to sit in
looking at the grass.

Waiting. There is a beach where you walk
up to your ankles in the water, wavering
on the pebbles, out to the headland, round
the last corner.

Waiting. The morning sea that says,
All streets lead here, and this is where it
isn't any longer your face that hides
waiting.

This too is the night's business.

EMMAUS

First the sun, then the shadow,
so that I screw my eyes to see
my friend's face, and its lines seem
different, and the voice shakes in the hot air.
Out of the rising white dust, feet
tread a shape, and, out of step,
another flat sound, stamped between voice
and ears, dancing in the gaps, and dodging
where words and feet do not fall.

When our eyes meet, I see bewilderment
(like mine); we cannot learn
the rhythm we are asked to walk,
and what we hear is not each other.
Between us is filled up, the silence
is filled up, lines of our hands
and faces pushed into shape
by the solid stranger, and the static
breaks up our waves like dropped stones.

So it is necessary to carry him with us,
cupped between hands and profiles,
so that the table is filled up, and as
the food is set and the first wine splashes,
a solid thumb and finger tear the thunderous
grey bread. Now it is cold, even indoors,
and the light falls sharply on our bones;
the rain breathes out hard, dust blackens,
and our released voices shine with water.

EPIPHANY, TALIARIS [1]

Wind smoothes the wet trees earthwards,
loud. In here, breath comes
slow. Same air; same what?

Flat leaves, a starry floor. Which
is the one that stands
still over a birth?

Sudden movement: leaf or bird?
For a moment, damp
soil escapes in light.

---

1 Carmarthenshire, former home of the Gwynne family.

MATTHÄUSPASSION: SEA PICTURES

1.   *Kommt Ihr Töchter*

Wind lurches down, pushing the thick sea like blankets,
scraping its breath on wood that rocks to sunken
pulses, and we are out of sight, over the other side,
cords trailing, slipping into travel: the hills under the sun
have shrunk, corners and sharp shoulders soften into grey
without horizon, where the wind's wet palm caresses

Dangerously. Between night and day, between light;
the fleshless hand slaps each cheek suddenly
in turn, the questions come in cold skilled voices.
Who? Where? The answers have been left behind,
in the fields under the sun, and the stir of wet grass,
the morning smell, der Bräutigam mounting.

Birdcries in level steps climb up the sky,
an icy stave, they say *this voyage will be with injury
and much loss.* Swell, cloud and ice, fire
running on the masts, the knowledge no one mentions
of bleached sightless wounded things
surfacing, water streaming down their awakened flanks.

2.   *Erbarme dich*

Look into ice. Force the wet fingers
squeaking against the surface, sliding up into
the little interrogatives of some tiny
animal. And the glass silence holds, your face
is held, floating against the dark, the backwards
world we shall never get behind.

We never get behind the dumb denying stillness.
Not I, not I; and the glass says, Just so,
not I, and when you look into the mirror,
you know a lifetime's words can add up to
no more than this, Not I. The soundless stranger
in the dark looks back, blank and protesting

That I shall never come to him unless
I break, push down into the water and the quiet
while light melts round the string-tight horizon
and the small cries fold inside my floating skull, and I
embrace, wide-eyed, the spinning depths
slowly, white cheeks puckering and soaked.

3.   *Gebt mir meinen Jesum wieder*

There are islands where we do not land.
We thread our way into the winter archipelago,
the empty shining castles, turrets and alleys,
and hope we shall avoid the rock on which, naked,
red hair frozen to the ice, he sings
as the current heaves him towards a final north.

Nothing to say but loss, he is his own
storm on a flat sea, words fast, blood slow,
and on his island's shore there is nowhere
to anchor, nobody to visit. He flings his words
at us like coins grown dull and smooth
from being clenched in sweating hands day after day.

We ease away, crossing ourselves, our faces
flaming abruptly as we begin to search
our pockets, empty them over the side; with pure

sharp little sounds, coins bounce over the floes
and waddle down the freezing midnight water. What
must we pay to get out of jail? says the gabbling fiddle.

4.   *Wir setzen uns*

Back to the headland fogs, exhausted
with new grief, old treacheries, the view without prospect,
rain falling in a slow afternoon, between light
and dark, no questions any more; the long grey
leaving of the day that never reaches night; the turning
water that will never carry us to the pole of sleep.

White nights; *wir setzen uns* in some unwelcoming chair
to wait. Scored down the sky, the neighing
of a car alarm, night's horses running sluggishly,
and then the unquiet of the muffled room as it bobs
on a frustrated tide that never breathes out, never
jolts into the wooden warmth of dock.

Wood, pulsing unevenly with a tired surge
as the fire fades; five o'clock cloud and damp,
clogging the throat. Slowly the line is drawn
again, tight between sea and sky, though not
where we remember, settled after the night's
fast-running sweats. With the dawn, sleep soft.

RESURRECTION: BORGO SAN SEPOLCRO

Today it is time. Warm enough, finally,
to ease the lids apart, the wax lips of a breaking bud
defeated by the steady push, hour after hour,
opening to show wet and dark, a tongue exploring,
an eye shrinking against the dawn. Light
like a fishing line draws its catch straight up,
then slackens for a second. The flat foot drops,
the shoulders sag. Here is the world again, well-known,
the dawn greeted in snoring dreams of a familiar
winter everyone prefers. So the black eyes,
fixed half-open, start to search, ravenous,
imperative, they look for pits, for hollows where
their flood can be decanted, look
for rooms ready for commandeering, ready
to be defeated by the push, the green implacable
rising. So he pauses, gathering the strength
in his flat foot, as the perspective buckles under him,
and the dreamers lean dangerously inwards. Contained,
exhausted, hungry, death running off his limbs like drops
from a shower, gathering himself. We wait,
paralysed as if in dreams, for his spring.

Piero della Francesca's Resurrection hangs in the civic hall of Borgo
San Sepolcro, Tuscany.

CAROL

Frost scratching at the door,
blood has spilled across the floor;
soldiers step down the hill,
weapons fixed for the kill.

Where is this? When?
Here. Again.

Light cuts across the floor,
blades of wind slam back the door;
pray the child stays still,
tighten at the sudden chill.

Where is this? When?
Here. Again.

Past the dismantled door:
dust and linen on the floor.
He has left for the midnight hill,
to hold the troubled planets still.

Where is this? When?
Always. Again.

FIRST LOVE ON THE WALL

Pouring, a steep grey snake, over the contours,
a shield, a skin, the little horns
that stand up, blinking, for surveillance
every few miles; silence; wind.

Northward are the moors, the forests,
wolves, stags and haunted lochs,
the naked folk with messages
carved on their skins.

Behind, the long roads into sun,
vines and boats, the metal wheels
and locks of victorious argument,
the common tongue, the taxes.

And now the talkative scarred skins
are here, the woods and water;
when I turn round, the Latin diagrams
and vines have vanished.

New messages rub up against the wall,
graffiti cut by walking woods
embracing, scratching, painting, wetting
the grey horned hide.

No road backward, now, only north,
to the sun in the dark loch,
the wine in the barbarian tongue,
the duty-free economy,

The common frontier, skin to skin.
The towers look blankly up and down,
nothing behind, only dead languages;
not even room here for the wind between.

PECKETT STONE WOODS

Fir-sifted, the wind is thin,
cautious, but its nudge
still bends the wood. Crack.

No answer to the knocking.
The wooden gong folds
down again, work done.

The woods near Trellech, Monmouthshire.

SENSES

Touching
The first task: to find
a frontier. I am not,
after all, everything.

Hearing
Inside, hollowness; what is
comes to me as a blow, but
not a wound.

Seeing
A million arrows, I
the target, where the lines meet
and are knotted.

Tasting
The strip of red flesh
lies still, absorbs, silent; speaks
to all the body.

Smelling
Not only servicing the lungs, the air
is woven, full
of needles.

Each door from the room says,
This is not all. Your hands will find
in the dark.

IN MEMORY OF DOROTHY NIMMO

Louche tongue and steady eyes and crisp
rejoicing teeth, she settles in the grass,
presenting breathlessly a penfull of bewildered sounds,
smartly pursued and nipped, fenced but still heaving
to a boil. This is no ordinary trial: you need
to chase the flesheaters, not just the browsers,
to hold the wolf and lamb in one fold
for one long minute. A short triumph for the bruised
lungs, but the prize is not in doubt. She holds
the eyes hard, a friend (if not man's best) still.

Barefoot, down the long woodland corridors of frost,
over the needles, walks the forgotten
mistress of the king. She smells of grapes,
candles, black furs, of cooking smells
and smoke in a cramped flat. She will disturb
the clinical forest air with haze
and trembling. In the shining kingdom,
in the rich winter malls, she opens for business
with a stall of odds and ends, cheap and irregular,
and scented with a lost indoors. *Don't beg*,
she says, *from the rich, only the poor;*
get absolution from the sinner, not the saint.

ALONE AT LAST

The room is booked for me, my mother,
my last four girlfriends, me at eighteen months,
my anima, you when I met you, myself
at sticky sixteen, you as I want you, you,
you in my ambiguous dreams, me as you want me,
me as I think you want me, your father,
you at seventeen after opening night, the boy
you spent it with, Darcy and Rochester,
the man you made up at fourteen with your friends,
giggling, God and my favourite cousin. Quite a few
more have said they'd like to be there, but
there's Health and Safety to think about, after all.
What if I shouted, 'Fire', to see who runs?
Or maybe just your name, over and over, until
it sounded stupid, but brought us, muttering
excuse me, spilling things, treading
on toes, into a space the size of sixpence, the size
of an eyeball, just big enough to hear
each other breathe? Love is, I suppose
the word that has to wait till then,
if ever, till the sixpenny width of breath overheard.

THE ROOD OF CHESTER
(after Gruffydd ap Meredudd)

Cut from the flowering tree,
the body sails by night
over a scouring sea,
stained red and white.

Monday at dawn, between the walls and the sand,
they saw the carpenter's masterpiece, delivered
out of the winter country on crowned waves.
The clouds' siege lifted and the rain sailed home.

Polished as bone, the oak comes through the storm
alive, fingered and pressed by winter after winter,
rolled on the gulls' table till it swims clear
between the walls and the sand at dawn.

They climbed down from the walls to see
the winter's carpentry, the skills of a far-off land
where they speak only the gulls' tongue; they walked
the noisy strand, one eye still on the white waves.,

One eye on the wind's knives. What else has winter
to deliver? The oak is spread like wings,
an eagle five times speared as it drops
out of winter between the walls and the sand.

From Adam's sandy grave
blossoms the magic rod,
stacked in the Temple's nave
to wait for the nails of God.

There is no gift like this for a city,
no wood but this for the roof, the bloodied wings,
the salted timber. They hauled it from the sand
and wrapped and hung it in the dense rafters, singing.

And like that other image form the shore,
at night its belly cracked and the men began
to scramble out, the men folded
into the eagle's wing, the men and women devoured

By its five hungry wounds. It has gathered
all who have left their walls, who were lost in winter,
on whom the towns have closed their doors;
they will make the foursquare City of the Legions

A camp of little fires for the homeless
where they sing unfamiliar songs in the gulls' tongue –
until the legions douse the hearths and take the ground again
and carve the oak into a whipping block for bad boys.

When the children weep
at their corrected fault
the clipped bird stirs in sleep
tasting remembered salt.

HEADWATERS

A knife's indentation in dough, wavering
across the moor, the blunt-nosed banks,
the grey and yellow and the polished stem
twining down, spreading on a plate to warm,
gather and melt another path. Listen ahead:
crusts stiffening, voice deepening, and the cuts
reckless, the long negotiation over rubble,
sounding like the disturbing, crystal,
unreachable voices that upset your dreams,
the language you will never follow, composed
by your sleeping self. All hanging on the bright cleft
between the swelling unbaked moss, up there,
the fold into the secret, the unreachable science
flowing raw from the cut earth on its back.

SEAMOUTH

Push push, it says, the midwife to a foreign
uncomprehending girl who hasn't even
worked out she's pregnant yet. And
Wash, it says, slapping the stained rocks
tearfully. And sometimes, Rush;
the pouring sand says it is too late,
you have forgotten where you should have been.
Brush, it demands, hand over
the tools for picturing and colouring
and tidying; they are not allowed. Hush. Hush.
Nothing you say is heard down here
as the moon's cords twist and pull
and the spray flies up; as the rock drops
and explodes in sparks, in glowing ash.

'BLIND PIANIST', BY EVAN WALTERS

Here is the left hand feeling, excavating
for the supports (the left hand
that in the East makes love and can't be used
to eat), the left that fingers origin and dawn, the sudden
opening lip across the darkness where day starts
building; the left hand cupping itself around
the bass's foetal curl, delving inside the coils
for the shell's echo, hoarse and damp. The left hand
runs up and down the pillars, a hand of strings
and hammers, a cat's cradle of drawn veins;
this is the hand that reads at night,
that touches base.

NAVE

I

Blown in their shadows on the glass screen,
the gulls invade, the sun projects them,
heavy scraps moulting from some looped black curtain,
the sudden darkness flickering; it makes you
shake your head, praying the brain is not yet
interrupted, that the thick industrial murmur
of our circuits and processions won't after all
attract the dropping wing of what may not
(so we suspect) be nearly as light as it looks.

2

Feather or paper, on its way down the deceptive
verticals, what are the choked gullies that it has to
navigate, the overcrowded passages, packed
with breath, words and draught? And still, feeling its way
along the crooked shafts and hollows of dead sounds,
there is no other destination for it but here, in the space
between our feet, still restless, shifting with every
breath, but caught, never able again, now it is here,
now it has managed the stubborn air, to leave.

WESTERN AVENUE

They always looked to me then like faces:
the square hat and the long sad barred eyes
and the tall teeth of downstairs windows, grimacing
in the hopeless well-swept everlasting ·
afternoon, the tundra spaces, drifts
of hours piling like newspapers in the corner.

And so the furniture is recognizable, the glue
for the construction kit and last week's Eagle,
abstract designs on the formica table,
patterns from the electric fire on the ceiling
through an asthmatic night, the gable
raised in surprise over a stunned window.

Somewhere in the first decade, a world assembles,
sad eyes, fixed teeth, the grey moorland inside
littered with glacial debris. The flat faces still tease,
recalling how the pieces stuck together,
on the table's edge, how the lungs would seize,
while the houses were dealt out like cards for ever.

LOW LIGHT

Black with the afternoon sun behind,
the branches steadily walk upwards, a trail of ideograms,
while the sun lifts its own long brush, breathing out
from the field's edge, whitening the earthward surfaces.

Turn from the winter glare to the bald, tall
barley sugar twists that stretch and yawn,
and the sun's brush insists they are green,
a rising blush under the drab bedroom skin.

The sun has turned the world upside down,
blowing the snow from soil to settle under boughs,
decanting the grass essence upwards through bark funnels:
it shakes the cold globe before it breathes in again and sleeps.

NEVER WASTING A WORD...

Never ransacking the tins piled
in the bunker for the final war, so that
we shan't find ourselves silent in the dark?

Never producing the tough plastic mass
that won't biodegrade and can't be used again,
squatting triumphantly under the squawking gulls?

Never leaving visible on the plate
the stuff that you can't swallow, stuff
they'd be grateful for in hungry somewhere else?

Never spending scarce cash on the unnecessary,
unswallowable, unrecyclable, unprocessable
once only offer? Or what?

COCKCROW

Dark and cheerless is the morn
Unaccompanied by thee.
Joyless is the day's return
Till thy mercy's beams I see.
CHARLES WESLEY

1.

As if light's arrival
were a brick splintering windows;
as if it were
bones poking in the gullet,
pushing it out of shape, so that
the retching cry falls
from the beak in a cascade
of fractures, rubble, shredded flesh;
as if day's return
were a running knot against the throat.

2.

Suburban children never hear it; so
the sound belongs for me with weekend
mornings in the valley; my aunt's bedroom
with the striped curtains, looking straight
towards Bethania across the road. Saturday,
empty hours and unfamiliar second cousins
dropping in. The puzzle as the slow day starts,
why does the sun rise to what sounds –
to the child's suburban ear – as if
the flesh were crying with a predator's sudden dig?

3.

Bring the two bits of wire unsteadily
together, and the light crows
broken and sharp between them; today
and yesterday and before
are shakily joined up, the jagged
current of words or pictures
jumps back to flickering life, convulsing
the cold channels, telling me
I've used up another cistern of supplies, so
the light blinks and flutters that bit more.

4.

And waking is to swallow
yesterday's broken glass;
to try to digest the bones
of words lying still
in farmyard dust, to hear
the rasp of cord running
down towards the neck:
how else should we greet
the predator that is
our shadow choking us?

5.

Or, cold and confused, we never noticed
the darkness thinning out, the fire turning pale,
the faces losing warmth, the bones
showing, the waterlogged flesh; so when
the sun's eye catches, it is the shock
of a noose thrown from behind. Down
on our knees we go, grasping the hemp
so tight the bones poke through, as if
this were the rope let down from mercy's beams
to lift us raucously into the fresh splintered air.

1.   *Romeo and Juliet*

Drunk in the dark, they toss the shiny loops
of silk back and forth, tottering around the pinnacles.
They trip and giggle over the tiles, they dare and shout
as the web crosses, spike to starry spike, and they
do not quite see, drunk in the dark, the little knots
twining around their feet. Tongues slur, eyes cloud,
limbs become heavy; the dream clings,
a wet cloth, over faces. So, when it gets light,
there is a web draping the Gothic spears,
damp, streaked with blood and silver, fading
as it warms. And the words caught in its circles
fall to the grass like fractured stone, like crumbs
from broken towers, tiles from the roof,
leaving the attics cold, the windows streaming.

2.   *A Midsummer Night's Dream*

As it gets light, the dogs sniff the wet scent,
and everyone stares, blinking, at an unfamiliar face.
All through the night, we have been chasing someone
who didn't look like that, we have been
mouthing and grunting strangers' names; now
we must find how to talk into the prose
of daylight, how to explain last night's words, the blind
desperate explosions in the forest, the long dark paths,
the tunnels where your hands feel fur and bone;
now it is time for moulding fingers on flesh rising
wet in the dawn, plaiting the shelters of shared gestures,
the eye's spark, the lip's twitch, the reminding
touch on the arm, the private smiling code, now
serious games begin, when magic has gone back to bed.

3.   *Twelfth Night*

Such a long journey. Will all the shipwrecks
and the stealthy night-time break-ins, the false beards,
borrowed tights, songs with the words you can't remember,
money for toys, dropped rings, corsets and swords
pay for the one epiphany? Kneeling in the straw
they all cry, What you can see and hear is not
the truth; I need to tell you, all you need to know is that
I never found the words. You can be drunk
with booze, bereavement, righteousness,
until your tongue swells so that you cannot even speak
your name. M.O.A.I. Cracked and dismembered,
letters drop in the path, not to be read, the gold
and frankincense are thrown away, the eyes look
somewhere else. A cold coming, raining every day.

4.   *Much Ado About Nothing*

Home from the front in time for cocktails; as if
among the balloons and fancy dress, death, terror,
betrayal retire gracefully to a back room, where they
play amicable dominoes till the carriages are called for.
No, not so easy; the disinherited chauffeurs shift and complain,
and drift, bored, one by one, into the party, switching
masks, voices, privacies. And the clear streams
and clever ripples catch and tear. All the prince's horses,
and all his men, will labour, pulling the wound or stitching it.
Words that were once the flashing cards
covering the table fall in drumbeats; heavily, heavily:
paper cuts can kill. Under the game's scattered tiles, the words
scratched on the wood read: Lose. Lose if you want
to live before the telegram arrives: Back to the front.

5.   *Measure for Measure*

Only the middle of the road is paved; on one side
the whores, towering in wooden pattens, navigate
mud and night-soil; on the other, the sisters
and the friars walk barefoot, with the stink
under their soles. The paving stones fragment,
thin out, disappear, and the loud voices from each side
close in. From each side the damp waste spreads,
and joyfully the friars and whores pile trick on trick,
because this is a game where you must break
the rules to win. Alone, in the middle, standing,
tearless and pale, the two survivors, who
want shame, silence, sleep, justice, nakedness.
They look from side to side at the excited solvers
of problems. Remind us. Who found out the remedy?

6.   *Antony and Cleopatra*

Smoke, powder-scented warmth, the long haze of the indoor
Toulouse-Lautrec late afternoon, the lipstick on the cups
and well-thumbed glasses; what you don't expect to find here
is purity. Because this isn't going anywhere, this
isn't furthering the general good, this isn't even making
people happy. Locked in the hazy lounge, they only want
to play and argue. All around the awed spectators ask,
How can we scale the Alpine heights of pointless joy under
the afternoon clouds, where the call to come home never penetrates?
Don't worry. Wait. The silver bullet that will break
the cups, mirrors and ashtrays is being forged out of
that other purity, forged for the reasonable man who is not
hurried by his blood, who knows by instinct just
the one gesture with his thumb to turn the raging current off.

7. A Winter's Tale

The white cells flower in the bloodstream, images
of her, the dream of someone else's bed;
morsel by morsel she too is eaten up,
cancered and cancelled. Under the ground she goes,
and he is left, dreaming in fever of the empty beds.
There was a man dwelt by a churchyard, dwelt
in the neighbourhood of children's leprous gravestones,
boys and girls dead in the great frost. One day there is
an idiot fairground music; spring working loose.
Women return to see the king's waste land, the dry beds,
and the blood flows again, fresh as cut grass, the white cells
colour, a dead boy stands up silent, a lost girl
sees her strange parents for the first time, stones
move from monuments. Pins and needles. Life, unconsoled.

8. Othello

I was made so as to listen: a white cloth
drifting, caught for a moment on the spines
and green of this or that man's great tumbling
story, made to wipe sweat and blood earned elsewhere,
spread for the imprint of a face: Veronica's
veil, but it is not someone else's death
that stains the handkerchief handed, man-to-man,
pricked, blotched and coloured, thrown down,
pulled between fists. Now I must listen to them
slapping my story down like cards, man-to-man,
until the table is pushed over, the white cloths
drawn, the last grace said. And I can see from here
the crumpled napkin stuffed in the mouth, silencing,
as my dead mouth absolves: Nobody: I myself.

9.   *Macbeth*

The muscles twitch, the skin crawls, all night long:
try again. Try to sleep, try to discover
the last orgasm that will take you into quiet,
the muffling of the itching mind. And each
new thrust will only coil and hone the nerves,
the lockjawed fluttering wakefulness. Be innocent
he says, of the knowledge, dearest chuck, withdrawing
slowly into an empty nursery. He sees her
playing with the dead child. She must be fed
with silences, tilts of the head, averted eyes.
Between them, through the itchy darkness,
move the unspoken things. As they drive desperately
at knifepoint into each other, they will never say
what each sees in the empty room over the other's shoulder.   .

10.   *King Lear*

It does not keep you safe; it does not
give you the words you need, it does not
tell you how much to pay, how much
they owe you. It will not work, like egg-yolks,
to cool the numb heat of lost eyes and treacheries.
It does not surrender to the reasonable
case for not risking everything to keep
secrets and rivals, the white line in the tickling
membrane of freedom. It will not keep you dry: rain,
like crying, sinks down to the bone.
It will not stop: not when you sleep, not
when you wake, not when you want it to,
not when you want to settle with the mirror
of your shame. Never. It will not. Never.

Translations

SIN

Take off the business suit, the old-school tie,
the gown, the cap, drop the reviews, awards,
certificates, stand naked in your sty,
a little carnivore, clothed in dried turds.
The snot that slowly fills our passages
seeps up from hollows where the dead beasts lie;
dumb stamping dances spell our messages,
we only know what makes our arrows fly.
Lost in the wood, we sometimes glimpse the sky
between the branches, and the words drop down
we cannot hear, the alien voices high
and hard, singing salvation, grace, life, dawn.
Like wolves, we lift our snouts: Blood, blood, we cry,
the blood that bought us so we need not die.

(From the Welsh of D. Gwenallt Jones)

LENT

A train steams into
the long tunnel. Windows up and latched,
doors checked against the rush,
the nightfall of soft smuts.

Dark, soot, smoke –
this is our luggage to carry under the single fading lightbulb,
pale ash on the tongue, sacking
over the fuel (flesh and soul).

A hard tunnel, narrow
for our crowding lusts, but there is nothing
for the soul's fingers to lay hold of
unless all is let go.

Out we shoot now
into a white expanse, lighting faces that have forgotten
hope. Westwards, the horizon colours:
over the hills' cranium, a red Christ sinking.

Three days' silence, dark,
the jolting seats, every hour endless.
So what shall we say, amazed, when the dead sun
turns inside out for morning?

(From the Welsh of D. Gwenallt Jones)

CHRISTMAS EVE

Who says we've got to suffer
with the thorn's splinters gouging,
when there is such a star, and such
a scent, roses and donkeys?

Who makes the stars shine so,
glowing like roses in the dawn?
Who warms the frosty night to be
a sable fur round the king's shoulders?

Here in the stable, no befores and afters:
just the heart's wild excess and the wisps of straw.
What in the end binds us to one other? The cross?
No. The child's birthcord.

(From the Russian of Inna Lisnianskaya)

MUSIC

I'm on this diet; only someone's really keen to do
the eating and drinking for me:
a savage music, drawn from the winter's day
and the flat peat marshes.

Shamelessly greedy, it's just not the kind of guest
you take with you to dances:
it's going to squeal like a fishwifely house-elf
and break the crockery.

The waiters bring its cocktail, wine and broken glass,
a whistle for its lips, so that it can
let out its high-voltage scream, an icicle
sharp down the wires.

It fuses all the lights, crunching away as if
with mouthfuls of croutons and nuts.
It sounds like the ice-crust breaking on the marsh.
It sounds inside me.

(From the Russian of Inna Lisnianskaya)

FOR AKHMATOVA

This is where treason and forgetfulness
mingle, like conscience and disgrace.
But she arrives, the Simple, the Arrogant,
to shake me out of bed each morning.

And I'm all over her with questions: where
is there now for us to go, and why?
 Why do we gather scorching roses,
weaving them into scourges for our breasts?

No, this is no self-conscious women's thing,
it's not some Shi'ite flagellation ritual –
only why, why do the words we venerate and love
set us, day after day, on fire?

(From the Russian of Inna Lisnianskaya)

FOR TSVETAEVA

Your bed has given up its load now you have gone;
and you can't take your time there any longer.
While we're still here, there's time enough to think
about our lives. For geniuses are born to offer dignity
to nobodies; while nobodies are born to reprimand the geniuses.

(From the Russian of Inna Lisnianskaya)

FROM THE FOURTH FLOOR

My look-out is the mountain peak of the fourth floor;
the eyes are flooded with desert, a seascape
with Bedouin tents blowing full-sail across it,
a mackerel sky, layers of quivering sea-foam.
We came here once together.

The sun has set. A stark white outline tells us
yellow moonrise is on its way, because
the sun and moon don't get divided here;
but you and I do; here's my soul
making a detour of a thousand miles

Round through the Moscow blizzard, where your wheels stuck fast
for good. You left your stick for me, to use it for
a compass needle, and I followed your direction
straight away. Off for a month or so to Bible lands, and never
letting my gaze wander from the sands and their remembering.

Dates blaze in clusters on the palmtrees, eucalyptus
scratches its side against the thorny aloe, and a voice
has been, all day today, crying in the wilderness,
sounding just like that creaking lift in Moscow: just the two
of us, a kiss exchanged as we went up.

Climbing to this fourth floor peak is hard work. But
the desert keeps going up into the sky for ever, you can't tell
camels' humps from clouds up there. And like a car
slipping into its garage, the pine casket slips into this landscape.
The real view's your death; my life is the mirage.

(From the Russian of Inna Lisnianskaya)

AT THE JAFFA GATE

Yes, my old king, my Solomon: still here,
your Shunemite. I can see your muscles have dried up –
not your eyes, though, sharp as ever, stripping the veils from all
you see. Can you strip my veils from me, as you survey
the grassy slopes, the rose-tinted vineyards, full of identical old crones?

You wouldn't know me now, not even naked. My belly's corrugated sheets
of sand. My legs used to bend like green moist twigs; not now.
My breast's the crumpled date left on a dried-up palm,
my veins trace patterns through my skin, clear as dragonflies' wings.
I wait for you sometimes, you know, by the Jaffa Gate.

Never come near you, though. Why bother my lord the king?
Beauty is what is exciting in women, mind in men. So waiting,
after years of post-coital cooling-off, I'm hot again
suddenly. It was the songs turned me on, not just the hard flesh –
and the one song, of course, that stripped naked love itself...

My God, you roused me - through my ears, my head...
and my hair, you said, looked like the sun's curling locks.
Any fool of a herdsman can screw without spirit, but it's not
how you get the blood bubbling like water on the boil,
it's breath to make the heart fly up, ripe dust from the peach blossom.

What you said to me I sucked and nuzzled, a bee in pollen.
How could it be, my Solomon, my old king, that the song –
the one that no one found till you – came back in your old age,
simpering and cheap, and made you vain, an empty stranger,
flat on your face to some imported golden calf?

I turn away from you, praying each day and night
for you. With love. The evening settles quietly, and I
light seven candles for you, stick them in a tray of sand,
rip my old shift and scatter ashes from the stove
off my grey hair. God save the king, I say. God damn the golden calf.

(From the Russian of Inna Lisnianskaya)

THE OTHER MOUNTAIN: RIDING WESTWARD

March, sun and haze, five o'clock,
travelling west; and the cloudbank sets
firm ahead, another range of dove-grey
slopes, great waves suspended dangerously
over the nearer ridges, thrown up by some
grinding of plates on the sea bed and held,
tight as a bowstring in a photograph
of disaster just about to fall. The quiet mass
waits, the hill country without paths or stones
or grass, it drives down behind everything,
tucking its bulk into the mountain's back.
While dark melts into the spring haze,
the road draws nearer to that corner
where the hills meet; when the button
is pressed and the tape plays and the wave
falls, there is no path or stone
or grass, no root, no standing, the pale bodies
drift, lifting a hand to ask for leave
to speak, compassionate leave, always to be
compassionately refused.

FROM CARN INGLI
for Waldo Williams

1. Master Class

The children in the school yard run
to hold the old man's hand.

They hold the hand that ploughs,
like Dewi, stony soil.

Where words will settle, germinate,
build homes for fugitives,

For the lost children far beyond
the yard. He holds their hands,

He feels the silk folds, thinks
will his plough-hardened thumbs

Print on the silk the skill to carve
leaves for an open door? The children

Hold the engraved memorial hand,
lift faces for inspection,

Steer him into the school to meet
the other teachers for their gentle sentence.

2. Exit Tax

The Western shore is what the left eye sees,
where the headlands of the senses join up
into one frontier: I am a body, this
is an island. Furious or still, what sits
on the foreign side has no words in common.

Shores where day ends, light is pinched out,
where the hand feels in vain for a wall
not there and the foot misses the stair.
The West is where the dead sail; the blistered
slopes, the cloth-smooth pastures, the beds

Of the burns unit, waiting for the drop
into sleep and water. In the left eye's landscape,
some futures are not possible: the ones
where I rehearse the deaths of strangers,
where I sit back, president of a tribunal

Where all the questions have been silenced
and all the enemies are underfoot. The eye
of the headlands opens wide, and foreign
tongues from the neighbouring darkness sound
in curlew cries of mockery. Nothing is owed

To futures of terror. Better to write
on the cell walls a few green words
that the left eye can recognise. Good news:
the only tax you have to pay is death,
not fear, not insurance, not obedience.

3. A View

What is nightfall?
The two grey millstones meeting,
grinding the sweet furnace-bright berry, so that
the juice leaks out across the closing mouth.

What is daybreak?
Clay lips unsealed, a glimpse
down the long lane of moisture gathering
under the skin of the unconscious hours.

What is the shore?
The debris of an argument
between the level grammar of the sea
and the wild singular nouns of stone.

What is the word?
The swift, fired from a bowstring
buried in fern, against the padded walls
of quiet streaming upward from the hill.

What is the voice?
The single line as the hill crest swells,
the liquid brimming in its improbable meniscus,
on the edge, always, of dark streams falling.

What is pity?
Walking up into the colonnades of rain,
tasting the water and the running mucus as you grow
cold, knowing the skin is no defence.

What is peace?
Down in the nest of roots fumbling
for drink, a pouring without end
across the bruised dark sand.

4. Monument, Mynachlogddu

To shoe a troop of horse with felt:
stealing across the dry, resisting grass,
but not with mounted men, not

To break in to nightbound camps
and put surprised half-naked conscripts
back to sleep for ever, but

Beasts of a Quaker apocalypse,
with no authority to hurt, padding
and stopping on the soil that

Springs like a ballroom floor, soft and
dishevelled, keeping their sympathetic distance
from the stone's still eye.

Sliced clean as marble; a glassy mourner
bending to read the blunt letters, the routines
of leavetaking. But glass will splinter: ragged bites
stand open and the port-red ooze, crusted
like scale in kettles, wanders, slow as a winter fly,
across the arctic slope. Gashed bodies
push out their sickness through the skin:
the marble mourner has leached up the fevers
from the rubbed lives piled round its roots,
sucking the moisture of the leaf-choked, rust-throated
fountain forgotten in the wood, the well
of loss, wounds, endings, seeping out
under the prosaic stones, clouding the glass,
cracking the ice. The tree of discharge.

CALDEY

The bay's mouth swells, sucking the gale
and spit into stone lungs, laying
the ground for what the island tells, hoarsely:
before the boats arrive, after the shops shut.

Beach

Sand shuffles amiably, like familiar words
stroking and nosing one another, melismatic
chant that slips and pours so quickly
that you never see the razor shell until
you feel grains rubbing the red flesh.

Coppice

Under the trees, the muttered conversations
of rain on leaves, wood, mast; dreams of pushing through
a restless crowd in this foreign town,
wondering what they suspect, what they fear,
what you look like to their glistening eyes.

Lighthouse

Bullets of water in the grey morning,
a lash of rapid pain on the cheek,
sparks from the boiling cloud, water
lifted, water dropped, something dissolving,
not an asperges; maybe, though, friendly fire.

Headland

Gulls cry their little sickle sounds
nicking the eardrums, scratching at the sea,
pecking and fishing into the confused sea light
inside, alert for the shine that tells them
where they can hook up something alive.

Breathing out, the long flare of late sun
runs to the horizon, the mouth says hoarsely:
you can tell how high the wind is
by how still the birds hang.

HERMAN IN YSTRADGYNLAIS

The baked crust, humps, mounds,
streaked faces like the seams
bent sideways under the tread
of long hours; and it breaks
around the heavy shoulders, the surface
cracked for a second into white
liquid, a hot light beyond summer,
light from the steel-mill always
labouring under scorched soil
as the generations tread, tread,
into the dust, the gas, framed
for a second in liquid anger,
in a steel love the ovens cannot
dry. *Arbeit macht frei*? Not so; only
the labour of the hairline keyhole
surgery in the heaped dusk.

SWANSEA BAY: DYLAN AT 100

I.

A thumb drawn down, smearing the grey wash,
storm pillars float over a December morning,
the sun still tipping rocks with liquid
out at the headland. In the bay swells urge
this way and that; a dark patch swings
out from the sea wall, pushes the pushing current
sideways, the planes of water tilting by inches
under the lurid morning, heaving this way and that
beneath the mottled skin and pinching it into the long
blade of a wave, the knife under the cloth
ready to slice. Watching, you have no notion
how it all runs, the hidden weights swinging
and striking, passing their messages, hidden
as the pulses under the scalp, behind the eyes,
that sometimes pinch themselves into a sharp
fold, into an edge, as if the buried cranial dances
gathered themselves to cut, for a moment, at
the skull's dry case and break through in white curls.

2.

I sang in my chains. I listened for the pushing swell
of light in the country yards, the undertow
of bliss that still cuts at the cloth, at the bone,
at all the tired shrouds. I listened
for the tide retreating and the small lick and splash
of breeze on the trickles between corrugated sand,
for the silent footfall of pacing birds, processing
to their office. Beyond the bay, the infant-bearing sea
slips further off, the next room is quiet and the sun
whispers hoarsely. When I call in my dream for it,
my voice is small and the knife strains bluntly
at the knotted cloth. Watching the swell again
at whispering liquid sunrise, I have no answer
when I wonder how the world's sand runs
out of grace and the dark moods of the water
jostle each other; I cannot tell if they will gather
ever again, severing the milky web that holds me
mortally. Do not go. Now as I was

CAMBRIDGE AT 800

1. Landscape

The river swings slowly on the clay;
A track in the cloud chamber, the old road
of Roman ghosts and lost dominion,
fingered with grass and mud, still carves the fen.
The little shrines of clunch and rubble sit,
shuttered against the needles of a draught
that treads the cloud chambers like a legion.
As if the first settler here was winter,
a slow craftsman of the shining wires
and filigrees, laying bright frost on black soil.

2. Divinity

Frost on black soil: when the first clerks,
wrapped tight, caps drawn down,
first intoned the dry music, blew on the sparks

And rolled from the furnace the glass spires,
twined close and polished hard,
the castle of the schools, they kindled other fires,

Slow-burning, flaring at last around the boards
of White Horse Tavern chambers,
as the restless Word scorched off its cords.

But the scrubbed reformed sky still yearns for motions,
deep vortices, storm towers,
for journeys into Plato's paradise, devotions

Like the draught's needles piercing the glass of sight,
stitching philosophy
into close music, into a formal velvet night

Of bowing constellations. Hung on the walls,
two centuries' worth of weaving,
the warm needlework of Greek that calls

The clerks to stir and dance again with the Word's
soundings, returnings,
filling the sky's towers, nesting and circling birds.

3. Natural Philosophy

Nesting and circling: vision catches
this or that landing place, guesses
this or that current down which to glide,
maps out the architecture
of stone and air alike.
The eye in flight, steadily as the river's
curved arm, traces a single horizon
behind the crenellations and the little shrines,
and a young Christ's man steps on board
for the long voyage to damp islands
where the forms heave out of water
inch by inch into defining light.
Back home the sculpting wind cuts deeper,
frost cracks down to the joint
of bone and marrow at the heart
of matter, the split anatomy of power
flowering for life and death. Life's letters
are decoded, rescued from the floods
of blood and breathing, hung in dry waterfalls,
stuttering an episodic song, the marks
and pauses of an aboriginal art.

4. *Humanities*

Marks and pauses: where we cannot speak
we must not, where we can we must,
and watch for the dishonest leak

Of casual silence where the white drifts
would bury needful, spare, unsparing words
of scrutiny; or of casual talk into the rifts

Of emptiness that mirror the uncrowded sky.
Power tends to corrupt, the patriarch said,
casting a patient, unmerciful, Germanic eye

On the soft histories we love to tell
(as if our past were beautiful and frozen
in what we say, locked in the cell

Of our control). Even in the cold
marshland, there is the heat of protest:
this is a critic's landscape, shaped to hold

The black no less than the bright,
and the sharp stripped trees no less
than the water: night

Where the stars' little wounds drop streams
of slender clarity, no less than days of mist
and the mumbled theatre of waking dreams.

5. *Townscape*

Waking dreams: across the lakes
of glowing grass, the wedding-cake
pinnacles drape themselves with ice.
Into the nest of grass, timber,
Tudor brick and stone, the straight
fen tracks run silently, treading
like a legion. Yellow-grey houses,
small clay ovens against winter,
stare at the postcard castles from time
to time: quizzical, grateful,
suspicious, knowing they are needed,
shrugging at the mind's obsessional
drive to forget where it belongs
and what it owes. And the Roman roads
fortify themselves in glowing glass
where the academy as it passes
reads silicon reflections. Roads, houses,
river, ice-framed sanctuaries,
all of them framing the human eye
discovering the human eye
within the human eye's fathomless black soil.

DOOR

Lift the stone and you will find me;
Split the wood and I am there
Gospel of Thomas

A book falling open, the sliced wood
peels apart, jolting for a moment
over the clenched swollen muscle:
so that, as the leaves fall flat
side by side, what we read is the two
ragged eyes each side of a mirror,
where the wrinkles stream off sideways,
trail down the cheeks, awash with tears,
mucus, mascara. *Split the wood*
and I am there, says the unfamiliar
Lord, there where the book opens
with the leaves nailed to the wall
and the silent knot resolved by surgery
into a mask gaping and staring, reading
and being read. Split the wood; jolt
loose the cramp, the tumour, let the makeup run,
the sap drain, the door swing in the draught.

ROADSIDE/VIATICUM

Blisters of rain on plastic wraps around
the flowers, the curling flowers with their life
peeling away steadily: *upon such sacrifices*
the incense is in short supply. Flowers
for a thankyou, for a last-minute birthday
present for your mum, for an embarrassed
girlfriend. Death, smiling and nodding, says,
It was no trouble, or, lips pursed, it's nice to see
how thoughtful you can be, or else just grins and blushes.

When you wake, crying, what you want
– failing your mummy – is your teddy. When
you go through the lethal crash barrier,
we cannot tell you when it will be morning
but we can give you memories of desperate
innocence to cling to. Death, always a soft touch,
says, Ah: sweet. I like it when you just get
used to it, savouring the tears in the sodden fur
and cloth. Saves you the trouble of getting up.

At the road's edge, we mouth like children,
blisters of water on our faces, lips
and limbs trembling. Left behind by the family car,
we wait under the rain, over the peeling flowers,
trying to remember why we mustn't
jump into cars with strangers. Come on, says death,
no point in standing in the wet. And you can stop
looking for more than fur and flowers, as if someone
were coming back for you from beyond the crossroads.

STATIONS OF THE GOSPEL

I

All music twisted in one string:
reach out with your long nail,
touch. Listen.

II

Poured from this stone, the water
stings, the mind lurches, suspects
joy, chaos.

III

The wind passes
no sentence: carries scent, sound,
a face felt in the dark.

IV

Thirst drops in the long
dark, swallowed cold by the eager
earth-streaked water.

V

In the deep pool
what fish is wandering through, to make
the dead limbs ripple?

VI

Bread's flavours: sand,
grass, salt, stone, blood, an open cut
from the shore's litter.

VII

Hands close on absence,
on broken waters from the cave
beneath the ribs' vault.

VIII

Before all journeys
there is the desert sky, glass-
clear, ice-resonant.

IX

Light catches the slicked
sand, ash, glances behind shut
eyes, opens a wound.

X

No no. Dusting away dazed
flies, he forces the lock;
snow blows in.

XI

Acid tears fall, corrode rocks
in foam, burn away
in shock the grave's knots.

XII

The bowl glows in the furnace.
Inside, the beads of sweat
spit and scatter.

XIII

On the worn shiny
boards the water runs, salt with
refuse from dark roads.

XIV

Door swings in the wind:
empty path, low sun ahead
blinds, slows steps, welcomes.

XV

Knifelike, the spring gales
peel skin from sour flesh shrinking
from the candid sun.

XVI

Long secret ends: blood-
smeared, a crown breaks the heaving
of the body's sea.

XVII

Stand here
before the mirror where you see
only the sun behind you.

XVIII

Splinters on paving
stone, red smears; through the window
foreign words stumbling.

XIX

Behind the soldiers' backs
the cloth tears slowly, soaked, eaten
with sour wine.

XX

Put your ear to the crusted gash
in stone or flesh; the mouth
speaks your name.

XXI

Catch it, catch it. The lake
brims over in the bright dawn,
runs from my hands.

NAGASAKI: MIDORI'S ROSARY

The air is full of blurred words. Something
has changed in the war's weather. The children
(whose children will show me this) have been sent
to the country. In the radiology lab,
Takashi fiddles, listening to the ticking bomb
in his blood cells, thinks, once, piercingly,
of her hands and small mouth, knotting him in
to the long recital of silent lives
under the city's surface, the ripple of blurred Latin,
changing nothing in the weather of death and confession,
thinks once, in mid-morning, of a kitchen floor, flash-frozen.

When, in the starburst's centre,
the little black mouth opens, then clenches,
and the flaying wind smoothes down the grass
and prints its news black on bright blinding
walls, when it sucks back the milk
and breath and skin, and all the world's vowels
drown in flayed throats, the hard things,
bone and tooth, fuse into consonants of stone,
Midori's beads melt in a single mass
around the shadow with its blackened hands
carved with their little weeping lips.

Days earlier, in Hiroshima, in what was left
of the clinic chapel, little Don Pedro, turning
from the altar to say, *The Lord be with you,*
heard, suddenly, what he was about to claim,
seeing the black lips, the melted bones,
and so, he said, he stood, his small mouth
open, he never knew how long, his hands
out like a starburst, while the dialogue
of stony voiceless consonants ground across
the floor, like gravel in the wind, and the two
black mouths opened against each other,
Nobody knowing for a while
which one would swallow which.

TO THE CITY

1. Bosphorus

Once there were chains between the towers
shackling the green-black forest walls across the water
locked in each other's mirror-gaze, chains to choke off
the galleys headed greedily for the tense city. Not now:
this is a motorway shining with oil, the lanes
jostling and humming with their relaxed freight,
birthdays and anniversaries and conference excursions
bouncing and rocking along the cleft so confidently
you could forget the swimmers dead in the green-black
depths, the ones who failed to breach the walls
on the far shore or break the mirror. And the day trips
swing round and land where they began. But in the unquiet
morning dazzle, the dolphins arch and plunge, unannounced,
bright needles pulling threads between air
and sea. They stitch their trails round the lethal cruisers,
the crates of oil and spinning blades, come without call
or cause, go without mercy. Out of the green-black vaults
the thread leaps, wavering in unquiet light,
to tow the boats out of their channels, draw
shore to shore, face to face, swimmers to gulls and sailors.

2. *Ayia Sofia*

And that, the Greeks tell you, is the Conqueror's black handprint,
when he rode in over the ten-foot depth
of corpses; when he leaned over, pushing
the half-globe on its axis, swinging the arrow
towards a new, south-eastern, pole. The bars of light
lie angled silently, rolling against the tilted bell:
a tongue's thread cut. The foliage of immense
words painted curling and waving, unmown
green verges of a scoured field, drifts across open mouths
and scratched eyes, the layered dead
under the flaring frozen seraphs. There are no hours
to strike, no consecrating whisper to be marked, where death
so rolls and stacks its fields. Handprints of soot
inside the burnt domes of skulls; the empty segment
on the sundial, where worlds have pulled apart
and shadows stand unmoved, the clock's hands
are nailed still, the bell cracks open to a sky
of frozen stars pointed in accusation,
flaring on spikes, burning for the uncountable names
harvested by conquerors for this or that revelation's sake.

3. Phanar; the Patriarch's Cantor

Anastas. Leaning back, lifting elbows, braced,
jaw out, he curls fingers and lips, to make
his brassy diaphragm a bowl where the round gale
swings on itself, brushes the metal to a shine. Fingers
unfold into the quieter pulsing of a sandy breeze;
the drone shifts with a grind, brows are wiped,
a tired eight-year-old begins to cry, is hugged,
scolded, bundled behind the screen. The wind
starts rising once again, the couriers pick up speed
and ride into the gaping caves, the lifting wind
scrapes sandy flanks against the bowl of lung, sinus,
damp and bone. What does it carry, the straining
weight searing his arms against the stall's wood?
The creak of stones shifting on the hill; forests falling; a body,
massive, limp, released from its ropes around the mast,
struck dumb? The windy grains ringing half-audibly,
bouncing around the bowl's rim? He lifts
his palms again; welcomes the rising, the stone,
the grain, the body, the little pestle
drawn round the bronze. *Anastas.* Lifted.

FELICITY

She is like a doll: not a doll given by father,
or an old doll from your big sister. Like a doll
I gave things to get from a travelling man.
Blood is what I gave to get this one,
shouting in front of them, shaming us.
How will it be, they said, when the animals
come to eat you, how much will you
shout then? I say, I will be like
the doll then, I will be someone else's, bought
with the blood and noise of someone
else so I don't have to.

They bought me like a doll
from a travelling man, the man
who took me after they burned the town
when all the blood and shouting of my father
and my mother paid for me to live.
They bought me, a doll for a little girl
who is rich and pretty. Year after year
she plays with me. Her little brother
dies, his face eaten up like by animals;
her big brother puts his hands on me
to push me down and pour his stuff inside,
and I get ill and strange, the blood stops then starts again.

She is going to be married, the pretty girl. She is
not happy. She talks a lot. One night
I must go with her to a bath in the dark,
it is a secret, there is an old man
talking a lot, I will make you free,
he says, and puts his hands on me
to push me down (first I think no, no) and pours
and pours water like my brother would
when we were little by the pond, and I
feel like laughing: father, he says, son,
magic breath, now the old ladies
will give you new clothes. Her too,

She laughs and shivers, it is a secret,
it is not like the other secret when he comes
to push me down. There is a wedding,
then there is a little boy. Now says her brother
you would like one too, laughing, and pushes
harder and I get ill and strange again,
and the blood stops and I become fat; they say
bad words, but she holds me and shouts
at them, leave her alone, she is my sister.
Sister? Her father says, quiet; sister,
like you have been together to the bath
in the dark, yes, she says, yes, do you want

Me not to call things by their right name?
that on the floor is a pot; she is
my sister. The he shouts and goes to hit her
and then he crumbles up and cries
and scratches his face and blood comes,
and he says, now they will come for you,
think of me and your brother and the little
boy. Her hand holds me tight and hurts
and hurts. Now she has no little boy
in here and I have my girl that I
bought with all that blood, and she tells
me dreams, how she climbs up

A ladder, every step between knives,
I think of climbing sharp strings,
like on a harp, and every step cuts
just at the moment when the note sounds.
And she dreams her little brother,
with his eaten face, so thirsty, but she prays
and his face comes clear and he puts it
into the pond and drinks and drinks, I think
of my brother in the sand by the pond,
cut all over, so thirsty and he cannot move,
and I think of the travelling men and wish
them thirst till they cannot speak.

And there are gardens, she says, old men
who smile and give handfuls of new cheese
and apples, and there is when she turns
into a man by magic and she throws
big men on the floor so they cry
and scratch their faces. Every morning
she tells her dreams. Now it has come,
what we were waiting for, we sit
on the sand, but there is no pond here.
I am ill and strange, my breasts are wet,
and everything is streaming out, streaming
into the sand and someone shouts and bleeds.

I watch. My sister puts her hands on me
to push me up, broken dolls, their faces eaten,
lie round, their faces thirsty, thirsty.
What do you have to pay to have
a sister or a brother? Like you pay
blood and milk for a baby, something
pours and pours out into the sand
and never stops, so you can hold
a hand and in the end you are not
someone else's, you are where
your sister lives, she is where you live,
you both are in the river washing the eaten faces.

YELLOW STAR
for Mother Maria Skobtsova

If we were true Christians, we would all wear the star
Mother Maria

Take down the star from the treetop:
after these two millennia, it is jaundiced,
scorched, its points still sharp enough, though,
to draw blood. When it first shone,
it lit the way to killing fields. It has not
lost its skill.

Pin the star with its glass spikes
over today's selected carriers
of the infections clouding the future's
blood. The star has made the rivers bitter,
bitter, the scorched neighbours cry out
with burnt tongues.

Pay for the star with forged certificates
of baptism, papers of citizenship securing
the right to emigrate from Christendom's
collapsing planet; hold up your hand
where the points have caught and drawn
polluting blood.

Step out, star child, into the queues
of neighbours lit by the lethal sign;
take bitter food and drink from the hand
of neighbours who pay the long price for being
there, always, under the light when we need
guilty strangers.

Hold up your hand; the star-drawn blood
binds you into the stranger's place.
While the light lasts, think how it is
that the dust of burned stars, the immeasurable
dust travels darkly over light years to reassemble,
alive and moist.

PLEASE CLOSE THIS DOOR QUIETLY

The slow, loud door: pushing against
a mound of dust, dust floating
heavily in a still room; step
slowly,

Stones can deceive. The ground looks
firm, but the dust makes you blink
and feel for purchase. This is
marshland,

Difficult light to sting eyes, terrain
whose spring and tangle hides deep
gaps, cold pools, old workings;
careful.

Too much left here of unseen lumber
dropped, knowingly or not, behind
the door to trip you while you rub
awkwardly

At naked eyes, opened on thick,
still, damp, scented air, imprinted,
used and recycled, not clearing up;
catching:

The weather of memory. Underfoot
lost tracks wind round an ankle
and abandoned diggings, wells, mines,
foundations,

Wait for your foot to find them,
drop you into the unexpected chill,
the snatched breath and swift
seeing,

The bird's flap at the edge
of your eye's world: things left
but alive; a space shared; a stone
yielding.

ALPINE MORNING (BOSE)

Fine snow, swift at dawn; eyes closed,
then afterwards, the flakes
broad and slower.

Bird's foot touches the cold branch: snow
drops on snow. Silence
touching silence.

Line falls from the split web, a single
snowflake clings. Whispering
magnets.

Water far off drips in the unseen
rock bowl: sound of stars
in the dark.

THE SPRING, BLACKDEN

Still. The hollow, green
and gold, and the flawless lip, promising
music.

The lip's note, level
frost, a ring to bind the falling water's
round blows.

Under the soil, humming,
lips closed till the frequencies break cover,
flower.

SHELL CASING

Lying back broadly, arms flung out,
curling like feathers; the blood has dried
now, and it is quiet in the wet, ridged bed
where only minutes back voice, flesh,
air split so loudly open. Now
work is over, others must take it up,
connect the tubes, wash things away, arrange
for labelling the anonymous flesh.
Curling luxuriously upwards, a hollow dove,
the body waits to cuddle to itself
the scrap of a small cry, of a large
emptiness, inside the frozen wings,
below the broad smile on a face
absolved, unfocused, long past hearing.

ARABIC CLASS IN THE REFUGEE CAMP
(Islamabad 2006)

One by one the marks join up:
easing their way through the broken soil,
the green strands bend, twine,
dip and curl and cast off little drops
of rain. Nine months ago,
the soil broke up, shouting,
crushing its fist on houses, lives,
crops and futures, opening its wordless mouth
to say No. And the green strands
stubbornly grow back. The broken bits
of a lost harvest still let
the precious wires push through
to bind the pain, to join with knots and curls
the small hurt worlds of each
small life, to say another no: no,
you are not abandoned. The rope of words
is handed on, let down from a sky
broken by God's voice, curling and wrapping
each small life into the lines of grace,
the new world of the text that maps
our losses and our longings, so
that we can read humanity again
in one another's eyes, and hear
that the broken soil is not all, after all,
as the signs join up.

BATWA IN BOGA

A wilting posy tied to his stick: heraldry,
like his plain shift, and the level of his face
more than a foot below us. How long
until we go home? Who knows we are here?
A few yards off his people have stopped
their buzz of not-quite-dancing.

We are dying here. Flies in a glass.
We are looked at here by the big folk;
who else knows? In the forest it is God
who looks at us. Out here he does not
see us, we do not see him. When
do we go home, out of the light
of your arrows?

There are, of course, says the UN man,
no pygmies in Boga. So no-one
is waiting to go home; and God in the forest
is content, of course.

Gently the channels close. Businesslike as ever,
the flesh deals with the shaking spirit,
blood goes, resignedly, in search of different
pathways, and settles in unsightly pools on cheek
and throat, and the air vibrates embarrassingly
through stiffened pipes. The turbulence is kettled
in the hot plaza where the ribs bend in the dark,
trees bowed by wind at night.
                     Thumos, the Greeks said,
anger is what happens in your chest, when roads
up and down are blocked, and the noise
gets thinner and the blood builds up behind
the dams, the kettle shrieks and rattles
on its flame. You cannot sing in anger: only when
a steady drum settles the pulse, and the police
go home, when it is possible to walk, steadily,
around the square where arguments are sifted,
and the passion flows, now loud, now soft,
like notes, a word, an answer, beating a path
through black lanes where the walls ring
as the feet fall and the music ricochets.

HOST ORGANISM

I have been living
under the layers
of grain and moisture,
earth in my nostrils
and the years ahead
sitting like hard
pebbles in my gut,
and the hands that get
to sift the slack
grit while I sleep
fearfully through hours
of gardening labours,
pull themselves clear
and scrape nails clean
so that I feel the pricking
of green points that seek
pathways and waking
and tomorrow's work,
pushing out of the seed
dropped by some unnamed bird.

HIVE

The empty garden fills. As you come
closer, the not quite silent wires,
the songlines, begin to weave. Walk
carefully: trip on the cords and who knows
what arrows might spring, what lethal
shocks arrest you, quivering, teeth
clamped, nerves flying. The tracks flow,
now, faster, into the drab house:
wait. There will be no invitation.
The long lines twine and crowd into the mouth
where the slow glistening boil
fills up the silence thickly. Somewhere
the messages are deposited, somewhere
the dust is brewed up into food and firelight.

WATERS OF BABYLON
i.m. Joseph Brodsky

Tomi

One of them sat by the Black Sea,
his tongue dry from its stillness, afraid
that moisture on the buds would drown him
in a flood of tastes remembered, in a chaos
of pasts slipping from their triste moorings; afraid
of the toothbreaking dialects around him,
the grinning mouths flecked with food
he could not swallow. By the salt sea
he dried and slept; salted, hanging.

Babylon

And another, peeling the willow bark,
nails stained with green shreds, to plait
a basket, to place in it the eggshell-delicate
hopes of the day when they too will know
how a future can be extinguished, crushed like eggs,
the songs recorded for a grinning themepark,
he weaves away, nodding and smiling at his audience,
and the fast drops leak like a darting tongue
from the basket, green as a snake.

Venice/Ann Arbor/Hudson

And another, walking by the lagoons,
by the campus lakes, the river at the street's end,
his hunger is too fierce, his mouth overflows,
the chewed fragments scattering as he closes
teeth on words from the world's other side,
grinning and shameless, paid (he says) to wear out
the patience of the young, the solemn, the embarrassed:
he eats and eats until he cannot talk any more, ginger
hot in the mouth. And the moist muscles swell and burst.

UNSEALINGS: SCHOOL PLAY
  for PW

Hand him a sealed envelope: a word
or number written inside to guess or maybe
see; the shape, like smoke, leaking out
to leave its smudges on the mind's sheet.

Tonight, though, it is not party tricks
for aspirant clairvoyants: you must hang out
your sheet against the wind of what my cold eye
expects to be consoling kitsch, singalong emotion.

Words handed to you; under the hot
light, what leaks out from inside the seals?
Shapes blossom into smoke, all that the words hide,
obsession, parents' guilt, loss, realism, all of the secrets

Stored up for you thirty years from now (please God),
drift from the page, smearing your sixteen-
summered eyes with smuts and grey water,
and I forget for a moment who you are,

Looking into the cloud of what you see,
what you are channelling, a hot mind steaming
the envelopes, baring skin to be scalded where
the dark thirty years ahead glances and spits,

All that you know, all that you cannot know,
your shadowed eyes and soot-flecked voice
parking authoritatively, for a few minutes,
the ready-made tricks, thrown without warning

into a foreign love, the accent of a feeling stranger.

WALDO WILLIAMS
Two Poems translated from the Welsh

WHAT IS MAN?

What is living? The broad hall found
between narrow walls.
What is acknowledging? Finding the one root
under the branches' tangle.

What is believing? Watching at home
till the time arrives for welcome.
What is forgiving? Pushing your way through thorns
to stand alongside your old enemy.

What is singing? The ancient gifted breath
drawn in creating.
What is labour but making songs
from the wood and the wheat?

What is it to govern kingdoms? A skill
still crawling on all fours.
And arming kingdoms? A knife placed
in a baby's fist.

What is it to be a people? A gift
lodged in the heart's deep folds.
What is love of country? Keeping house
among a cloud of witnesses.

What is the world to the wealthy and strong? A wheel,
Turning and turning.
What is the world to earth's little ones? A cradle,
rocking and rocking.

YOUNG GIRL

That was what the stone carcase once was, a girl;
each time I see these bones, she takes hold of me again,
and back I go to her haunts, with every year of mine
answering for a century of hers.

She lived among people who knew what peace was,
buying their goods from the earth and the earth's gifts,
wondering silently at birth, marriage and death, tending
the human kindred's bonds.

All too soon she was put away, in her eternal foetus-crouch:
twelve times she greeted the arrival of May, and then
began to keep company with the darkness that took her, her voice
no longer heard on the hill.

So that the wide sky became deeper on account of her,
the blue sky brighter on account of her, and
the unseen ageless house above the hill's peaks more firmly founded
on account of her.

A child's skeleton in the Avebury museum, from around 2,500 BC.

BEDTIME: FOR RMW AFTER TWENTY YEARS

You sit sometimes, watching them fall asleep,
sleepy yourself, impatient and resigned at once,
and out of nowhere come the pictures. Sitting
beside a well, waiting for the dark gulp
of a dropped penny. Sitting beside a stream
under the rain, watching the water build
and spill. Sitting beside the witch's fire where
the pan of spells shivers and spits, and pricks
a watcher's careless hand in the stories, so
that he claps it to his mouth and finds this kiss
has made him understand the speech of birds;
sitting beside the water, still or closing silently
or restless, running with talk, or boiling and painful,
the element of sea change, whale's radar and birds' speech.

A BROKEN JAR: FIVE WORDS FOR MAGDALENE
(For Peter Relph)

1.

The world runs over: slow as paint
coursing down canvas, trailing
long stilts of oil, the ointment
runs into wounds still waiting
(dark flowers) to open.

Matting the hair, coating the hands,
pity runs over, sticks flesh to flesh,
goes out of town to meet the foreseen wounds,
eases its way into long wells of foreseen pain.
Pity.

2.

The world runs over: spilled
on the table-top, red streaks of wine
settling in wooden clefts like rockpools
as the sea drains off, wine to soften
the glistening edge of suffering,

The fear of hurts to come. The wine
runs over from the cup we share,
share to remember, share to forget
the darkness unplumbed in the well's long fall.
Wine.

3.

The world runs over: pressed
in the body, wounds leak out
and rise to flood peaks, rise
towards an Ararat where no birds fly.
The fountains of the deep

Are opened, life is eased over
the iron rim and courses down,
painting the flesh, painting the wood
in stilts and strands and in abandoned clefts.
Blood.

4.

The world runs over: stripped
from the sticky wood, the body
courses downwards as the tears
leak, twisting into the oil that wraps
the excavated flesh, the open mouths

Of the long wells. His cut skin parts,
an O where no words work,
and silence slides down on to earth
softened with clear pools after thunder.
Tears.

5.

The world runs over: sharp,
cold morning, when the uncontrollable
new sun breaks cover, runs across
the iron rim of the horizon, lucid
as tears, glowing as oil,

Dense as blood, dizzy as wine, a shattered
jar's scent drenching the spring air,
cups running over. Run, he says,
tell them now, tell them the sight and smell,
Mary. Mary.

CHARCOAL AND WATER: A LENT DIPTYCH
(for Celia)

Dense ash at night, the smoored fire
sleeping, a pit for the hands to warm
themselves: when the caves and tunnels
of the flickering daytime coals
and branches have collapsed, then you
can dip your hand and smear, Ash-
Wednesday-like, warm dust along
pale paper foreheads, to remember
where we shall all return.

Slow cold first light, the rain,
the drizzling bright mist, the dishcloth
sweeping the stones, leaving them pale;
leaves drop, light on the silver ground
where the ash drains blackly into corners,
and you can dip your hand and touch,
baptism-like, a young bone promontory
launching into the wet, remembering
where we shall all begin.

MAMETZ

The twigs catch in the itchy cloth,
pins plucking insistently, young hands
that pick, cling, branches whispering,
Don't go, must you, come back soon,
I'll miss you: thorns like voices,
voices like thorns.

Flesh catches on the wood; *I saw
one tree hold in its branches a leg*, heads
caught by the hair. *Red against green*, leaves,
the dark, running; hot snapping shards
plucking insistently, pinching a life out
here, a life there,

A jaw, an eye and half a stomach,
the black wood pecking, small claws,
whispering, Don't go, not ever, whispering
under the white and deafening blanket,
Stay here, I'll miss you, with each
dip of the black head.

They hang in the trees, *not a tree unbroken*,
long coloured capitals, foliated, streaming:
name after name after name after
name, cut in the wood's torn page,
cutting the itchy fabric of statistics,
writing; red.

REGARDING A CHILD
Vingt regards sur l'enfant X

        after hours listening
to the lap of tides forward,
back in the new lungs, sounds
in the corners of untried
flesh
        your eyes slip,
widen and quiver, folds of skin
like rasping blankets, the light
uncertain, it sometimes melts
in black flowers on to the
earth
        rain-slicked and straw-
littered, bedroom walls dissolved,
the half-dream where he lies
out of doors silent on some
stretch of dark wet
mould
        sunlight chattering
on leaves above where the black
pillars sink straight down
and down, or lost on the
moorland
        hooves cantering
in the flat scrubby distance
(as the gusts swell and retreat
and the webs shine in the morning),
printing the scores of
war
        on to the manuscript
paper, empty staves, where
the lines begin to slip,

stutter with failing electricity,
melt down on the
screen
         that hides the silent
    oiled pulsing of the machine
    whose lights flash like
    the flickery tails of coloured
    fish
         your eyes unable
to tell where and when the spark
flies, eyes open to the pricks
of flint shards, shrapnel
where the chisel bites raw
stone
         and the electric clouds
collide and clap clap
for the spark, pitpitpit
the rain falls on slow sea
rocking and slipping back to
sleep
         with him lying still
    hung round with loud
    fanfares, echoes of shouting
    echoes in your
    head
         of the lost places
the stone the fires
the shocks the deep water
the knives the hostile shore
the prisons already scored for
hands
         that reach in to where
uncertain light shows skin
that shines like the damp webs

at dawn and there is no
way of seeing what
eyes
            beyond the frail light
    see of the measures
    unperformed where the lines
    hold the colliding
    fires
        whether the rain
comes pitpitpit
on the stone flakes stinging
faces, whether what runs
from crown to chin is water,
blood
            or the warm
spread of oil, the terrible
anointing, making the wounds
glow, making the colours
flicker inside the
rock
            and on the shore
    finding a word to trace
    where the tides will not
    reach, on a dry
    sheet
            draped over pebbles
blowing a little with the wind
that melts and fractures
far overhead against the dark
the pale shape-hunting
drift
        like wriggling scrawls
down your rasped eyes
because after hours listening

the folds gather and the tides
stand for a moment under a
moon
     and wait to breathe out
  while your head falls
fathoms down into
the wood where sparkling
birds
    chatter as you walk
silently, the black pillars
mounting up and up, loud.
Loud. Then you
wake.

ALDERLEY: FOR ALAN GARNER AT 80

Edges: where we stop, guessing
the drop, the angle and the impact;
where a blade has driven down
with God knows what weight
of anger, longing or blind loss,
to carve letters too large to read.

Edges: where owls and snow drift
down , spill quietly and stifle
the long clefts where something once
was said (the little words
and their big letters), some hurt never
to be read, never to be levelled.

Edges: the clean, trimmed frame
where the blade flew through
the granite, where the longing
or the anger made a door
in the world's wall, in the hard
screens of time, of forgetfulness.

Edges: the single black walker
between snow and bellied sky,
between the caves here and the hollow
nightfall there, between the bone
and the star, a bladed foot falling
to cut the unlevelled path,

A story voiced from the long
letters in a stone book, here
but not now or then; the one
who sits down by the well's lip,
watching for it to open, for the memory
forcing edge from edge.

FOR ANTONY GORMLEY

(i) *Transport* (Canterbury Cathedral)

1.
As on the last day: a stone
slides sideways, and the long shape
floats, blind, virginal arms
tucked at the sides, into the hollow
arc gathering the pillars; then,

As on every day, halts and hangs.
From here the words haze up
around it, wisps of smoke, streaming,
nudging at it, tiny snouted
things pushing at a log

Athwart the river. Speak,
and a half-hour afterwards perhaps
you notice it, shifted a foot or so;
aslant between grave and sky, moved
but not yet flown home by all

The murmur from the tourists
and the altars, from the questions
and answers looking for each other
in twists and cross-flows, never
visible from the floor:

We can't see whether one
ever sparks another, flows in one
fast draining vortex into dark
and motionless homecoming,
nudged at last into the stream.

2.

What holds the long shape once
held up the vault: not flesh, not bone,
but nails, as if this body
of our aborted resurrection once
had been a great felt mannikin

For pinning messages and curling snaps
and numbers and reminders, and they
fell, one by one, on to the sinking
floor and the furred nap
peeled away in some unseen

Storm, and the metal pins
and bolts and tacks clung on together,
magnetised: the shape that rises
is the shape of all those sharp points
driving through numbers and postcards,

A smeared indecipherable stab
into a lost soft tissue, all
the body that will rise made up
afresh from the clinging metals
that opened casual wounds.

3.

Keep talking and the clustered
nails keep turning. Breathe:
the body shifts in the river's
leisurely flow. No drift
of wind blows off

Scale from the armature;
the only open eyes are draughty

gaps between lost messages,
lost numbers and reminders
turned in the creeping

Breeze from the floor we look from,
watching the dangerous body
hang where lightning's known
to strike. Holding our breath in case
it leaks and makes the spark, the river, leap.

   (ii) *Subject* (Kettle's Yard, 2018)

There is before, surely,
and behind, and underneath
feet planted, and the skull's
neat dome locking me in
between walls. Here though,
from one walled room
to the next, from
floor to ceiling, long rods
shine and travel, and the map
moves silently around,
down, up, the angles
yawn or snap, my skull
a bowl to dive in,
twisting and curled,
from a wet boarded
ceiling, or my feet
fixed to a wall, so that,
undomed, unlocked,
what is on top is
open mouth, hollow shaved face.

Whether behind me
is six inches or
thousands of empty fathoms
doesn't signify. Anchored
somewhere, all I can do
is lie on absence,
pushing my shoulderblades
down on the air's breathy bed
to dent it into shape,
into a holy shroud.

THE SHORTEST DAY

(On the fiftieth anniversary of the Aberfan disaster, 21 October 1966;
for Joseph Davies, Fflur Wyn and the Swansea Festival)

1.

Still warm from sleep; but the rain
seeps in. Greasing the pavements,
the rain seeps in, heaters are piled
with coats and gloves, and the metallic smells,
warm as sleep, slip through gaps
in the noise. Nobody knows that this
is the shortest day. Midwinter. Night
falls before the sun is properly up. What
I remember is a face still warm
 from sleep, I think of it smeared cold
with rain and then the iron woollen smell
around the noise, and then the cracked piano
and the hymns and the dismissal.
When the day ends.

2.

When the dark comes,
when the day ends,
and the dead lie down
beside their friends,

When the dust flows,
and the breath flails,
and the clock stops,
and the mind fails,

In the long time,
in the night dread,

when the cold
sings in the head,

Let there have been a second
before the weight fell
for a sense, muffled
like a passing bell,

A hand's touch, a hot
pinprick on the skin
announcing silently
a way in

To the last room,
to the last fear,
to say, Sleep now,
quiet's near.

3.
I get up now, I walk
to stand at the water's edge,
not believing
                there will never be
                your voice at the door,
                on the stairs again,
                in the garden;
I stretch my bitten fingers
over the water's edge,
not believing
                the day is over,
                that it ever began,
                that we woke up,
                that the rain fell;
I scan the soaking dark

for you as your face fades,
not believing

          we planned the weekend,
          argued about tomorrow,
          thought of this afternoon,
          of you grown up;

Not believing

          there is anything
          to say or feel.
          Anything.
          Anything.

4.

Paham mae dicter? why
is there trouble? What else
is there to ask, what else
is there but asking?
When the day ends,
what else returns

Filling the eyes with black,
yn llenwi'r llygaid duon,
black leaves, black dust,
black melted in falling
rain, the day's end like
a starless night at sea?

Where the water stops, clenches,
runs, stops, flows, beating;
you listen for the pulse,
feel for the tremor of a lung
labouring to pull all the waters
back over the still horizon,

bedclothes warm with sleep.

KHOI-SAN

The rising of the sun
And the running of the deer

> 'The Bushman... remains all his life a child, averse to work, fond of
> play, of painting, singing, dancing, dressing up and acting' (Dorothea
> Bleek, The Mantis and His Friends, 1924).

> 'The skirmish at Vaalbank [1855] was only one of many hundreds of
> raids, counter-raids and commandos raised explicitly to exterminate
> the San...Small wonder that the Qing "had never seen a white man
> but in fighting" (David Lewis-Williams, Images of Mystery. Rock
> Art of the Drakensberg, 2003).

1. Hunt

The beast trails its arrow,
runs, stumbling. At the end
genuflects, listing
over for the last
blow. Blood falls

from nostrils, foam trails
from lips.

          Eyes watch,
pools between slopes and shadow,
level under fast clouds.
Chest works, skin stretches;
the cellar floods.

(Think nuns staring
at a tabernacle,

eye to eye, without irony
or anger.) Beast's gaze
and hunter's locked,
one long breath on which
the beast sails
behind the stone.

Running,
running towards God's
home whose whereabouts
the fast herds know.
And bright smoke,
honey spirit, breaking
from the stripped skin
here, breathing.

2. Dance

Eyes water in the honey smoke,
swelling, a soft beat
on stretched skin; the old man
shuffles deeper into
the circle, the pit where the floods

rise, and a hot hand of iron
touches his spine, hot rain threads down:

face soft, loose,
so the foam trails and the blood
falls; he lists onto his knee,
breathing a path

Into the rock,
where long ropes silently

slide out, tangle him in.
Knotted and still, watch him
lifted, leaking the sweet stuff
from beaten skin.
          Pooled eyes running,
eland's eyes, circle the fire.
They bring the sick,

            he touches them:

Hot, honey-soaked, breath hauled
up from the cellar; pain
to touch pain,
here, shivering.

3. *Hunt*

Hunters come for the hunters,
their faces blades, their eyes
travel angrily. They force
the door, beating skins,
breaking locks, they find

stale bread, the four-days' old
dead scent. Then the stone

          Rolls shut to them
again, ropes hauled in, no wounds
left on the painted face. The new

Hunters bleed bitter salt
from their restless eyes,
while the waters run out
from the cellar, and the skin

wrinkles and the rain
stops. They do not
know why the whistling
wire is slack, the string broken,
and all around, the people
are leaving, trailing foam fast
in the air, running

With the eland to where
they know, to the wound
where honey rises
like the sun,
elsewhere, now, always.

POOL

A twig breaks. Promptly, obligingly
staging the haiku, one or two new frogs
plop in the water, where their younger
kin lie or skitter, hundreds
and hundreds of fat commas swept
from the compositor's workbench
into the sandy shallows, hundreds
of little fat breathing pauses in the water's
dull paragraph. When their breath
has pumped up shiny eyes and limbs,
they will wait too, throbbing by the pond's

Edge, listening for the crack of danger,
for the dry foot of this uncertain
upper world that no-one had predicted
back when it all was wet long soundless
clauses between the wriggle of black breath;
ready to leap from this new Purgatorial
height back into steady dark, away
(for a while at least) from the terrors
of what the sun sucks upwards –
green, limbs, lungs, even words
or wings.

LAST NIGHT
   (i.m Pamela Paul)

The nurse goes out again, he leaves
lights turned down. Against
the curtain she has settled
into a long ridge of hills,
the Malverns, say, on a clear
evening: a slope up
to the curved fleshless nose,
a sharp pull down to where
her mouth still struggles, folded
striations in the neck and collarbones,
then heaving upland, strong
slow gusts lifting and smoothing
covers, and a ruck of earthy
blanketed scree down to the bed's end.

After the flood, when the waters
slipped away, hilltops
will have shone, the hard
glow of rock when the sea
pulls down; oiled, anointed.
Skin shines as it pulls tight,
as the tide goes out, when
the flood is past, when
it is all over in the morning
and the nurse is back to draw
curtains half-way, and say
what little has to be said,
when what is to be said
lies on the floor, rumpled:

Water pulling away, a flat
stillness brushed with cloud,
and the beached drawn dry
silhouette with whatever
oil it is makes bodies light.

HERMITAGE, KENTUCKY:
THOMAS MERTON AT 100

Today what thunder smells like
is woodsmoke and dusty paper:
the trees burning slowly
for fifty years since the strike
of lightning that felled and split
the knotted growth of silence
dropping in a deserted wood,
and the smell lingers in cloth,
stone, books, the shabby
stool parked in front
of table, icons, and the cheap
grain of cinder blocks.

The tortoise by the path
looks dead (too much traffic of ants),
struck not by lightning
but by the strain of walking
in search of water. Coming back, though,
the first drops falling, all
the ants have gone and the tortoise
too, the thunder's smell like vinegar,
perhaps, pinching dead muscles
in a sneeze, burnt dust
scattering, as a foot falls again.
We walk on, wet, smells changing,

The wooden music in retreat.

CYPRUS WELL

(in memory of Charles Causley)

Sometimes it's a clock
ticking that punctuates
the stream of whatever
it is that flows
through a silent house,
sometimes (look across
the room), a fingered dance
tapping the white open
spaces with typewriters'
stiletto heels, sometimes,
from a line in a far valley
the anapaestic hooves
conjured by locomotives,
breaking the smooth iron
track into staves
and clacking feet. This
is the beat here: echo
of a steady voyage, fingers
tracking the pace of life
watched though these washed panes,
eyebrows raised, fingers
probing for the pulse
driving flesh and soul,
the thump of brief feet
over the skipping rope
out in the schoolyard, where
they learn to keep time

to their grandmothers' verses;
now, then, and now,
a hand moves up
to pull the cord:
communication?
as the carriages shock,
jostle and fall still,
silent like the house.

THOMAS CRANMER

Recycling parchment was a skill
you needed when the business
of book-making was expensive,
glacially slow: taking the pumice-stone
to rub the surface, shave it smooth
of the whispering filaments, the bristles
pushing through: scrape down to silence,
hold it before the firelight
to check its new nakedness.

After they dressed him up
in coloured rags and pointed hat,
they stripped him to his shift
again and scraped the hair off
from his skull and took a knife
to shave the hands of the last
lingering stubborn damp of holy oil, dry
and stubbled, he hung there, a skin
to write on, naked, old and fresh.

I never knew words could be
so ground and swept. What shall I cry?
After the stone's rub and the knife,
now I am held up to the fire?
He runs into the rain, slipping
on treacherous cobbles, praying the drizzle
would streak the skin again in black.
He puts his hand out, peering in firelight,
to sign a last will or a new testament.

UNDERGROUND NEIGHBOURS
(NORTHERN LINE)

I.

When they have clamped her chair, her face
(hot, patient) wheels up to the packed carriage,
ready to be washed or kissed, her hands
twitch and drop on knees, a flickering
accompaniment on the bone keyboard,
vamping silently. Brushwood tangles
bob at the green snag of rock as the water
runs on, accompanying, up, down,
over and over and under. That's it:
water catching the light; loops of repeating
shapes one by one, *da capo*,
face shifting on the stream. Sometimes
her eyes catch light and the wet spark
flashes; sometimes turn inward and the lips
settle, something like a smile. Lips
drawing back over teeth: delight?
distress? Perhaps she is accompanying
the awkward couple in the facing
seats, tattooed arms folded. Eyes
catch the light, turn in, turn on. Catch,
glisten. The water is quick, glassy, shallower.
The running tape wears thin,
the beat slows steadily, a solo crackles
in the last level fast passage to the fall.

2.

Heat peels back clothes and unembarrassed skin
faces the air, the secret messages laid out
for browsing; skulls, serpents, butterflies,
names in badly spelled Gothic, flowers,
crucifixions, hearts; flesh wrapped
in a cathedral's worth of signage.
The doors are open for the interested tourist,
though guidebooks aren't on sale. What moves
in skin (it seems) is older than you thought,
a long procession of the dreams that you're
supposed to leave behind, the crypts, the cryptograms
leaving their punctured trail, joining the dots
where the blood has dried quietly: the skulls,
the butterflies, the names that say
there is a story somewhere telling you
why the blood runs away, why the skin
loses its blush and dries, and you
have to guess if what is left is bone
or flower, someone else's name or
someone else's death, a stabbed heart leaking,
drop by fat drop, to join up wounds
or wash the buried dreams, puncture
locked cellars with a needle light.
Heat peels the covers, lays them neatly back:
Read me, you say, like a book, that is,
Slowly, uncertainly, turning back often.

DOLOROSA
(i.m. John Hughes)

The path is cold, feet slip
on the damp streets shining
with rain and blood. Someone has lit
small fires along the way and we
stretch out our hands to them
before beginning once again
the walk into earth and silence,
into the other city.

TRACK: THE WISDOM WINDOW
(For St Catherin's College, Cambridge)

The shore stretches; packed stones
give way to sand. Very far ahead,
someone with streaming hair and arms

Spreads to the light, hands driven
upwards and out at the water's
unseen frontier, pushed into light

As if by tightening veins in the branch;
pulled by the sun whose raw stuff
feeds the whole way from cobbles to sea's end.

Feel for the thin doorway, open
between the singing angel and the wordless dog;
they are your friends, still neighbours and

Still foreign, all through the scrub
and stone. They will run alongside
right to the unseen border, telling you

What you are not, while the dishevelled
words fly in the flatland gales, handholds
when you have come to the bleached rise, hunched

Very far ahead, where the hills
bow down like seraphim, couch
like dogs, under the glowing dark

Of hands, leaves, sand, rivers
luring the sun's raw pulse
down to our veins.

The wall leaves a gap, a grinning letterbox
before the thatch starts: steady light
pours smooth into the long mould, sets
in a beam, pivoting on the sill, tilting
by inches, slowly, as the thirsty darkness on the far
side of the wooded rise hauls it down
and pulls the bucket up out of the wide
fire's well. It hauls the smoke into the glowing
mould, packing it firm; sparks, scraps of ash
blazing like snowflakes, the smoke's column
a blizzard of sharp stars. The writers
round the fire feel their way, by inches,
hauled to their feet by the rising dark,
their words spat fast out of the whirl
of charred debris. Poems blaze in the glowing bar
of smoke, and disappear, grey in the roof.
And they sit again, the poets, sink
into the cooling cauldron. Hard to believe
that what they mixed, kneaded, moulded,
boiled is so quickly eaten in the shadows:
a short shining in the bright moulded smoke,
then the grey drift into evening. The poets
wonder, shrinking again to their benches,
how is it anyone believes where it all
started, before the long patibulum
lifted them up and out.

MILTON

What hath night to do with sleep?
says the demon, slipping behind
the bushes, always around a corner
of the wet, shrinking globe,
as milky oceans rise, pulling closer
curtains and girdles. Someone pushes
the stone round and around that will grind
things smaller, black grit between
the wheels of earth and heaven,
eyeless. The demon smiles.

Hands feel for hands, the warm
bread that angels *not manacled with joint*
or limb break in a slow afternoon
as the late paradisal light
lengthens across a future
streaming away from the garden's
foothills and marshes over the levels
where night begins falling. Fingers
search for the keys, the stops,
the strings; they wander all night
over cold sheets. *What hath night to do?*

Words gather at the forest's edge, awkwardly,
at the hill's foot. You can usher them
to where he feels for hands and bread, take
their husked grains to the mill, the winepress
of the wrath of God. Round and around
like *Hesperus and his daughters three*, but
no golden tree, only the sweaty vintage
that anger presses. Day shuts his eye,
and the broad fields are lost. But he stays,
standing, standing, saying and standing,
searching to see the tree for the wood.

EASTER SUNDAY 2020

The doors being shut

The moon's soft gong
has sounded somewhere, dawn
air padding at it, and the dense
flurry rises, prickles and liquid,
chit and purr, and the breath
of soil, grass, blossom, the dressing
gown, drapery not yet burned
off by hardworking heat.

Walk into it, the cloud
discovered only in this
cold space, walking a tall
man's length from the next
riser from sleep. This is
the cloud in which stones
grind fast, spark, and the first
fire jumps out above the sun.

Noli me tangere

I could have said, Don't touch
me; never mind the doctrine
mandating your distance, why
should you have the right
to probe and roam wincing skin,
browsing to find the little
doorways into familiar pains?
I don't want what I know,

I don't want thick air,
the breathless damp neighbourhood
of voices and beating words,
the cloud swaddling and rubbing
with old practised polishing
sweeps of a working thumb. A tall
man's length from me, do you know
how I want that?

Heart burn

Standing here, weather
moves through us, drifts
like microbes or like neutrons
falling, clouds of prickling
song or picking nails. A tall
man's length away, unmoving,
is the visitor, whether in touch
or not I can't decide.

The moon, rinsed to a shred,
dissolves. Clouds are sucked
upwards. Light turns raw,
earth dries out. So what am I
hungry for, the globe of shining
distance, for the palm
of breath and liquid sound against
the face, for the thin, thin

Unseeable gap between breath
and breath, opening and clenching,
where it burns so hard, so
quick you don't know hot
from cold or now from then
or I and it, the needle point
where the gong starts to blossom
and the air quivers with wounds and difference?

POST-VAX: SPLOTT COMMUNITY HEALTH CENTRE 2021

Face the wall. Fifteen minutes sitting
(are we there yet?). Muffled routines wrapped round:
numbers and dates of birth and reassurances;
fatigue; polite and weaponless fatigue-clad welcomers
steering. All afloat in the pungent stream
of gel, dense and meandering seaward as we stare
facing the wall, novices in the *zendo*, bristling
for the tread of masters with sticks; or teams
braced tight along the floor's hieroglyphs
to leap and land the ball.

Breathe out (are we there yet?). Feather-light
fresh infections drift without landing, weaponless,
through the air's rustling, where
numbers and dates and reassurances float,
while the wall looks back at us, a patient goal
that waits to be touched, waits like a gong for striking.
And in the drift and rustle, something has shifted, roots
loosening in the belly till we can almost
hear it: the body's tight pouch
silently punctured.

THREE POEMS BY EUROS BOWEN
(FROM THE WELSH)

The Word

In carefree carefulness over the fair
linen cloth of our words of praise
while bread is being broken for us
and peace shared in the word
about wine poured, given for the sake
of an age obsessed with planning
and performing tomorrow's crimes,
from the heart of this sureness of ours,
let radiant nourishment stream out
to feed the trust of men and women,
till its red dawn has its way, breaking
light out of the secret place, so that the word
of grace never grows and hardens
into an ideology of Christ.

Lazarus

No; there is not a thing he can remember
of how it felt inside the tomb,
or anything belonging
to that dead season,
only the noticing, as he woke up.
of memory whited out,
the memory of the unboundedness
of the last moment of dark sickness.

Breathing is pleasure, breathing the goodness
of wind at the cave's mouth,
listening to his tongue's surprise
as it comes to itself again
eating bread at the table.

He knows that what he died of
was familiarity, the same old things
day after day.

But now there is more than sound
in the noises around him, feelings
feel more, taste tastes more, smelling
is more than smelling. He cannot
hold back the smile, standing
at the back door, watching the boundlessness
of the almond tree whiting out the yard.

Panel on the Arts

There were four of us busy discussing
the arts. Poetry shouldn't bother
with girls or flowers, stuff like that,
in a world like ours.

That was the critics' considered verdict
over the pub table:

There's more important things for you
to focus on in a world like ours –
the language crisis,
global tribulations,
the meaning of life, and all the rest of it.

The talk moved on to this,
that and the other, the twists and turns
of life: it emerges one of us
is after a girl, another's newly into
rose-growing, and the third is telling us
the state of this year's mountain ash
is prophesying
a hard winter.

~ Notes on *Headwaters* (2008)

Sarov, August 2003: the Outer Hermitage
Serafim of Sarov is one of the most popular of Russian saints
(he died in 1833). He spent a long period of isolation in
the forests after many years in his monastery, to emerge as
a counsellor and wonder worker who greeted his visitors as
'My joy', and whose physical transfiguration was reported by
a close associate in a narrative that has become classical in
Russian spiritual writing. The site of his hermitage, and the
outcrop of rock on which he prayed in his soli tude, can be
seen near Sarov; throughout the Soviet era and beyond, the
city housed a centre for nuclear research and was a restricted
area.

Matthäuspassion: Sea Pictures
The sequence around Bach's *St Matthew Passion* uses the titles
of various items in the work – the opening chorus, the arias
describing the repentance of Peter and of Judas, the final
ensemble.

In Memory of Dorothy Nimmo
Dorothy Nimmo was born in 1932, began publishing poetry
in 1984 and died in 2001.

For Inna Lisnianskaya
Inn, Lisnianskaya was born in what is now Azerbaijan in 1928
and began writing poetry in her twenties. She was published
only in the late sixties, since when her reputation has grown
steadily. She has been compared – understandably – to Anna
Akhmatova, and her tribute to Akhmatova is translated

in this volume. I am greatly indebted to Professor Daniel Weissbort for introducing me to Lisnianskaya's work and to his translations in *Far from Sodom*, Arc Visible Poets no.14, Arc Publications, Todmorden, 2005 (with an introduction by Elaine Feinstein), though I have not invariably fol lowed his readings of the Russian.

The Rood of Chester

Gruffydd ap Maredudd composed his long poem (210 lines) on the 'Rood of Chester' in the third quarter of the fourteenth century. It celebrates one of the foremost pilgrimage shrines of the Welsh bor der in the Middle Ages, and makes use of the legend that the great cross in St John's Church in Chester had been discovered cast up on the shore of the Dee estuary. He links this with the mythical history of the True Cross, made from the tree which grew out of Adam's grave (in fact from the seed dropped into his mouth), which had also furnished wood for Solomon's Temple. According to one tradi tion, the Chester Rood, torn down and hacked to pieces at the Reformation, provided a whipping block for boys in the grammar school before being burned. The poem is one of the greatest master pieces of mediaeval Welsh verse, replete with allusions not only to the Bible and the apocryphal tradition but also to Welsh legend and literary culture. It is printed with a full translation in Barry J. Lewis, *Welsh Poetry and English Pilgrimage: Gruffudd ap Maredudd and the Rood of Chester*, University of Wales Centre for Advanced Welsh and Celtic Studies Research Paper 23, Aberystwyth 2005. The pre sent poem might be described as a variation on the themes and images of Gruffudd's work.

'Blind Pianist', by Evan Walters

Evan Walters (1893–1951) was one of the leading artists of early twentieth-century Wales, remembered for his vivid portrayals of local scenes and personalities of the Swansea Valley and elsewhere.

Sin

David Gwenallt Jones (1899–1968) was a massively influential pres ence in Welsh literary and intellectual life, as influential and iconic in his way as Waldo Williams and Saunders Lewis. The two poems translated here represent early and late work, reflecting the relative formality of his earliest poetry and the much looser, almost conver sational, style of his last collections.

~ Notes on *New Poems* (2021)

Several of these pieces were commissioned for specific events – in three instances, as words for musical compositions. 'A Broken Jar' was written for Peter Relph and the choir of Magdalene College, Cambridge; a version of 'Mametz' was set by Brian Hughes as part of his *Sorrows of the Somme*, first performed in Cardiff in 2018; and 'The Shortest Day' was commissioned by the Swansea Festival for a commemoration of the sixtieth anniversary of the Aberfan disaster in 1966, set by Joseph Davies as a sequence for solo soprano, and performed by Fflur Wyn. I am deeply grateful to all with whom I collaborated on these works.

In 2015, the pianist Cordelia Williams spent several months working on Messiaen's *Vingt regards sur l'enfant-Jesus*, and invited me to write a poem to accompany her performance. 'Regarding a Child' is the result; my thanks to Cordelia for the suggestion and for her outstanding realization of the Messaien sequence. Media images from September 2015 of the dead body of a refugee child, three year old Aylan Kurdi, on the seashore concentrated minds at this time.

'Charcoal and Water' was written for the catalogue of an exhibition of Celia Paul's paintings at the Adam and Rowe Gallery in 2015. 'Dolorosa' was composed to mark a ceremony of blessing for Lida Kindersley's Stations of the Cross in Little St Mary's Church, Cambridge, in memory of Fr John Hughes. St Catherine's College, Cambridge, commissioned 'Track: the Wisdom Window' as a meditation on the stained glass window by Thomas Denny (in memory of Neville Burston) in the College Chapel, installed in 2012.

INDEX OF POEM TITLES